D1554661

All Things Beautiful

All Things Beautiful

An Aesthetic Christology

Chris E. W. Green

Baylor University Press

© 2021 by Baylor University Press
Waco, Texas 76798

All Rights Reserved. No part of this publication may be reproduced,
stored in a retrieval system, or transmitted, in any form or by
any means, electronic, mechanical, photocopying, recording,
or otherwise, without the prior permission in writing of Baylor
University Press.

Unless otherwise stated, Scripture quotations are from the New
Revised Standard Version Bible, copyright 1989, Division of
Christian Education of the National Council of the Churches of
Christ in the United States of America. Used by permission. All
rights reserved.

Cover and book design by Kasey McBeath
Cover art courtesy of Unsplash/Joe Beck

The Library of Congress has cataloged this book under ISBN
978-1-4813-1558-6.
Library of Congress Control Number: 2021939841

Printed in the United States of America on acid-free paper with a
minimum of thirty percent recycled content.

for Zoë

Contents

Acknowledgments

It takes a village to write a book, and I am incredibly lucky to have so many hospitable and generous people living with me in this village. The folks at Baylor University Press, and Cade Jarrell in particular, have been a joy to work with throughout this process, from first to last. I do not want to take that kind of guidance and assistance for granted. I am glad to have partnered with them, and I hope what I have written is worth the effort they have put into it. As always, I have leaned on my family and friends, a number of whom have read these chapters in whole or in part, and have shared their responses with me. I need to thank Danielle Larson, Christopher Brewer, and Matthew Moser, in particular. Other friends, too many to name, helped me in other ways, including letting me talk through my ideas and reminding me to take a break when I was frustrated with my writing. I am grateful for each of them. I also need to thank my colleagues at Southeastern University, and Sanctuary Church, as well, whose constant support always means the world to me.

My happiest debt is the one I owe my family, of course. I wrote this book during the COVID-19 pandemic, and during a move from Florida to Oklahoma, which means, among other things, that I owe them even more than I usually do. For months, they afforded me all the time and space I needed, even when it was seriously inconvenient for them. My mom and dad let us stay in their house for months while we looked for a home in Tulsa. And day after day, my wife, Julie, and sometimes my kids, as well, listened without complaint to me reading through my countless drafts, always asking good questions, and invariably offering exactly the encouragement I needed to stay with the work when I was ready to call it quits.

Finally, I am dedicating this book to my oldest, Zoë, who has been a source of life to me and our family all of her life. Bird, it is a *delight* to see you flourish as a person and as an artist. I am impossibly proud of you and thankful for you. You are a gift.

Introduction

Art is not a plaything, but a necessity, and its essence, form, is
not a decorative adjustment, but a cup into which life can be
poured and lifted to the lips and be tasted.

Rebecca West

Art reminds us that we belong here. And if we serve, we last.

Toni Morrison

Our works have more lucidity than we ourselves do.

Jean-Louis Chrétien

In his *Modern Theology* review of Rowan Williams' *The Tragic Imagination*, David Bentley Hart admits that in spite of his admiration for anything Williams writes, this particular book bothers him because it comes "perilously close," he says, to a form of criticism that spoils whatever it touches.

> I tend to think that all great artistic accomplishments occur on the far side of a mysterious threshold where propositional or analytic discourses fail because they are infinitely inadequate to what lies beyond. Every true work of art is an indissolubly singular event whose intricacies can be approached only by a language in which the most tactful poetic phenomenology—of the delicate and of the sublime and of all the beautiful medians in between—has displaced every

1

form of explanation, whether technical, social, economic, moral, psychological, philosophical, theological, or other. When we try to reduce the work to the lesser languages of those fragmentary disciplines, all we do is retreat from the incomparable to the conventional, and from visions to platitudes. It is rather like attempting to understand the flight of a swallow by attaching anchors to its wings.[1]

Williams' understanding of the tragic distresses Hart, as well. The tragic is "more 'musical' (in the classical sense) than discursive." And its "aesthetic form" is "affective rather than conceptual, consisting in a certain overwhelming mood." Thus, Hart insists, to ask what it "means," to reduce it to its moral teachings, is to take its soul.

Thomas Merton says something along the same lines about our knowledge of God: "We can never fully know God if we think of him as an object of capture, to be fenced in by the enclosure of our own ideas. We know him better after our minds have let him go."[2] But if Merton and Hart are right, why attempt what I am attempting in this book? I am attempting to construct an ecumenical aesthetic Christology, one that both honors the Christian theological tradition and responds to the challenges and revelations of the arts. And whether or not my effort is successful, I am confident this kind of work can be done. Of course, God is never "an object of capture." But he is also not a God who cannot be touched (Heb 4:15). Thus, we know God not only in the letting go but also in the embracing, the grappling. And I remain convinced, in spite of Hart's warnings, that it is possible to write about that emptiness and fullness, as well as these gains and losses, without retreating from the incomparable or reducing the glorious to platitudes. Art, in whatever form, can be a sort of theology, as any theology can be art.[3] And art can open the way to God—both the making of it and the meeting with it. Why? Because there is an "inner kinship" between God's Word and our words, between God's creating and our making. And that inner kinship, and some of its countless and redolent manifestations, can be brought to words without deadening its truth—without grounding the swallow.

Theology, art, and spirituality are joined uniquely in the liturgy. The following chapters, therefore, are arranged to follow the progression of the Christian year, beginning with Advent and moving through Christmas and Epiphany (and the first stretch of Ordinary Time) to Ash Wednesday and Lent; attending to Good Friday, Resurrection Sunday, and Ascension Sunday before turning to Pentecost and the second, longer stretch of Ordinary Time. In this way, the book reaffirms among other things that God's life with us is storied (in both senses of the term), witnessing to the beginnings and ends, as well as the heights and depths, lengths and breadths of Christian theological confession, aesthetic expression, and spiritual experience. Christ, "the man for all seasons," is known whether we are gathered or scattered, in protest or in praise, in the day together and in the day alone, in sorrow and in joy. God is with us and for us—as we need, if not as we wish—so that we might take responsibility for what happens in his world, without ever imagining ourselves as saviors or taking on ourselves or imposing on others more than we or they in fact can bear.

It is fashionable, at least in some circles, to insist that art, unlike craft, is necessarily useless. But this idea rings false to me because of my own experiences. What Garth Greenwell says about his first encounter with the Slater Bradley painting that now hangs behind his writing desk is remarkably similar to what I feel about my first encounter with Enoch Kelly Haney's painting, *Emptiness Has a Claim on Death*, which knocked me off my feet when I was a child: "The experience I had viewing it was something like love, what the French call a *coup de foudre*, a thunderbolt, and I knew that I wanted to feel its effect again and again; I knew that it was something that would be, in some way I didn't fully understand, *useful* to me."[4] That never fully understood usefulness, which, in the words of the Welsh poet and artist David Jones, comes when "utilitarian death" is "swallowed up in the victory of the gratuitous," is at the heart of what makes art, art.[5] I am a theologian, but I was awakened to theology not by reading theological texts but by reading a novel—George MacDonald's *Lilith*, in a course on fantasy literature—and by a lecture on *Moby Dick* I heard in an undergraduate course. I knew in that moment that I had been changed, that a new future had opened in front of me, one I could not wait to enter. Whatever else it is, then, this book is part of the working out of that future, a way of honoring the debt I have to my teachers and the books they made it possible for me to read, and a way of provoking others as I have been provoked.

Because I wanted to provide an ecumenical aesthetic Christology, I have tried in the pages that follow to engage deeply with a wide range of theological sources and artistic "texts." For the most part, I have limited myself to poetry, fiction, paintings, and film, many of which are familiar if not "canonical." My approach, influenced as it is by Williams and Hart, as well as others as different from each other as Jean-Louis Chrétien, Simone Weil, and Toni Morrison, may strike some as "old-fashioned." But I remain convinced that if we give texts the attention Jesus teaches us to give all things—"take heed," he says, again and again—we will find that they continue to yield surprises, reminding us that the whole creation, including our artistic works, lives and comes alive in the light of what the Scriptures teach us about who God is and what God desires for us. As with the bread and wine of the Eucharist and the water of baptism, so with anything and everything we have made: whatever we offer as gift to God and neighbor, the Spirit transfigures for our good. God's very life is gift, a giving and a giving-back; so, our works are never simply what they are in themselves: they are what they are in his creativity. To say the same thing another way, it is more blessed to give than to receive precisely because in giving we receive nothing less than our existence, our humanity.

David Jones' long poem, *The Anathemata*, shows us that all human work, including the work necessary for our survival as well as the work of our worship, is from first to last eucharistic. "We already and first of all discern him making this thing other."[6]

For Christians, to be human is to be gifted and tasked with the capacity for taking what is, transfiguring it, and making a gift of that transfiguration to God and neighbor. We believe this because we have been thunderstruck by an image: Jesus, already burdened by the ordeal he is about to undergo, taking, blessing, breaking, and giving bread and wine to his friends. In that liturgical act, which recalled not only Israel's but also creation's past, he showed us how our making can and must become part—an essential part!—of God's creating.

Reading Jones' poem provoked me to write one of my own, a sort of homage. And so it serves, I think, as a fitting introduction to this book I have tried to write.

> Before I wrote these words, before I knew how to write, before my late mother signed my name for the first time, to my father's delight, before the Hurrian hymns or the cretic meter, before divorce scripts or gravestones or marriage seals, before tabulations or registries, before the first letters were formed, hastily, no doubt, and late at night, before a poet first felt the fevered lack of them, before a scar first marked a slave, a slave, before the first priest first lifted up a sacrifice with her praise, before names summoned either a face or a thing, before the mammoth-stalker's first whispered warning, before my first father's first call charmed his lovers in the morning, before the groan of grief, before the squeal of pleasure, before the first predictive gesture, before larynx or teeth, before breath and the bones of the hand, a word was there, just abiding, uncreated: a blessing, and not a curse. And I give it to you now, at last, like this.[7]

1
Painting a True Christ

Advent

Thou shalt not make unto thee any graven image,
or any likeness of anything.
Exodus 20:4 (AKJV)

Were there no Creator and so no creation, no standard world,
artists would need to do no work.
Robert Jenson

In the act of making, we are necessarily
delivered up to judgment.
Geoffrey Hill

Bells, Light, and a Piece of Coal

Terrence Malick's *A Hidden Life* (2019) is meant to be a revelation
of Franz Jägerstätter's martyrdom, a vindication of his sacrifice,
and a witness against the fear that such sacrifices are offered only
in vain. But in the film's one unforgettable scene, Malick, who is
notoriously reclusive, reveals something more about himself and
his artistic vision, a vision that is profoundly, wonderfully, troublingly christological.

Toward the end of the film's first act, the villagers in St. Rade-
gund, a farming village high in the Austrian mountains, sense the
surging power of Nazism. Some of them, like the mayor, exult in it,
drunk on xenophobia and nationalist fervor. But a few, including
Franz, and Fani, his wife, are repulsed by it, even if they are not

sure what to do with what they feel. In the fields outside the village church, Franz confides his doubts to his priest, explaining that he cannot comply if called up for service. The priest urges Franz to reconsider, pressing him to count the cost of his rebellion: "Your sacrifice would benefit no one." But in the following days, Franz refuses to give to the collection for veterans and their families, and refuses to accept the state family allowance, as well. These refusals provoke a visit from the mayor, who pleads with Franz to change his mind: "Show a little humor. Nobody refused but you. Please." And, later, a visit with the bishop ends much the same way: "You have a duty to the Fatherland. The church tells you so." Back at home, a friend explains why the bishop and the priests dare not risk speaking out against the Nazis. Resistance is futile—"We don't have a say. What can we do? We little people here?"

In typical Malickian style, this last question lingers in voice-over as Franz walks along the road toward the village. Passing a small crucifix on a pole, he looks back, suddenly startled, as if seized, and stares at it for a moment, perturbed. Once he reaches the church, where he must have gone to pray or to meet with his priest, Franz finds a painter, Ohlendorf, retouching the church's frescoes. Standing on scaffolding, the painter towers over Franz, and asks Franz to hand him up a piece of coal. As he turns to his work, Ohlendorf reflects on the vanity of his project: "I paint the tombs of the prophets. I help people look up from their pews and dream." He stops, and looks down. "They look up and they imagine that if they lived in Christ's time they wouldn't have done what the others did. They would have murdered those whom they now adore." He gestures toward the images adorning the ceiling: "I paint all this suffering, but I do not suffer myself. I make a living of it." Franz, too, looks up, knowingly, it seems, but says nothing. The painter continues, his face half in shadow. "What we do is just create sympathy. We create . . . admirers. We don't create followers." Church bells begin to ring, and Ohlendorf takes up a small piece of gold foil. "Christ's life is a demand. We don't want to be reminded of it." Later, outside, Franz sits on the scaffolding, staring out into the distance, as the artist restores an image of the holy family, and confesses his guilt: "I paint their comfortable Christ, with a halo over his head. How can I show what I haven't lived?" He turns, again, and looks down at Franz for the last time. "Someday I might have the courage to venture, not yet. Someday I'll paint the true Christ."

This scene recalls another in Malick's *To the Wonder* (2013). In it, an anguished priest, Fr. Quintana, distressed by God's absence and his own inconstancy, stumbles into a midday conversation with the church sexton, an old, white-bearded Black man, cleaning the church's stained-glass windows, large and small. The old man recognizes the priest's loneliness, and encourages him to invoke "the power" when he is alone. "You've got to have a little more excitement. Just like when you and me are around, you know, and there ain't nobody around. Just—Hey!" He jerks, and slaps his hands together with the shout. "The power hits you, brother. It always hits me. You can just say, 'Hey, power,' and it hits me. Or hits me before I can get it out." He bursts into a fit of tongues. "See, the devil don't know what I'm saying. And you won't know and I won't know." Fr. Quintana smiles and looks away, and the sexton presses his hands against the window. "I can feel the warmth of the light, brother. That's spiritual. I'm feeling more than just natural light. Feeling the spiritual light, see? I can almost touch that light, coming right from the sky." The priest places his hand on the glass, too, but says nothing.

These scenes both refer to Andrei Tarkovsky's masterful *Andrei Rublev* (1966), the story of the great medieval Russian painter's estrangement from and final reconciliation to his vocation, after a long and bitter trial. But unlike Tarkovsky's Rublev, Malick's painter and priest remain at odds with themselves, incapable of doing the work they feel they need to do. The priest, grim and joyless, lives in the light but never feels its warmth. The painter, condescending and aloof, despises both himself and others around him. He is "high and lifted up," but the coal in his hand does not burn, and it purifies nothing.

Grace, Necessity, and Imagination

Is Malick making his confession in his painter's words? Is he offer-ing a critique of his own or others' art? Perhaps. But maybe we should not take Ohlendorf's words at face value. After all, unlike the villagers and the mayor, unlike the priest and the bishop, he, intentionally or not, confirms Franz' convictions, assuring him that the way of the crucified is indeed the way that must be fol-lowed. Whatever his doubts, whatever his failures, Ohlendorf continues his work. And even if he does not always do it rightly, even if he merely "retouches" the work of others, work that is itself not fully faithful, he nonetheless bears witness to the truth. In the end, Franz himself becomes a "true Christ," and the painter's work, false as it was in so many ways, helped somehow to make that truthfulness possible, directing Franz' attention toward the reality by which everything else is judged. The painter's coal does not burn, but it reminds of one that does.

The same holds true for Fr. Quintana, who in spite of his doubts, or perhaps in some mysterious way because of them, guides his parishioners toward joy, helping them to find them-selves, to find each other, and even in losing each other, to find God. Just so, we can see in Malick's vision that the artist's vocation is a reflection of the priest's, and the priest's a reflection of the artist's. And we can also see that neither the artist nor the priest needs to be a saint or a master. That is, neither the artist nor the priest needs to be good, or even good at their craft. They need only to know that they are called to love the good; that they, with everyone and everything, answer to the good; and that the good answers finally for them.

Perhaps this is why Rowan Williams contends that artistic representation is above all an outworking of "obedience." The artist—whether poet or novelist, painter or musician—finds she simply cannot fail to answer to whatever it is that makes her work radiant and internally coherent. Hence, she does not "make up" something from nothing, but "makes out" what is already there, inviting a reality to unfold itself as she remains present to its unfolding.

> The degree to which art is "obedient"—not dependent on an artist's decisions or tastes—is manifest in the degree to which the product has dimension outside of its relation to the producer, the sense of alternative space around the image, of real time and contingency in narrative, of hinterland. As we noted with Flannery O'Connor, the artist looks for the "necessity" in the thing being made, but this "necessity" can only be shown when the actual artistic form somehow lets you know that the necessity is not imposed by the hand of an artistic will but uncovered as underlying the real contingency of a world that has been truthfully imagined, with its own proper time and space, its own causality and coherence . . . The artist is always concerned with things as they are in relation to something more and other than the artist.[1]

In a famous and famously difficult essay, the English poet Geoffrey Hill describes the "technical perfecting of a poem" as "an act of atonement, in the radical etymological sense—an act of at-one-ment, a setting at one, a bringing into concord, a reconciling, a uniting in harmony . . ." In Hill's judgment, the poet must work and keep working until the poem "comes right," that is, until the poem shows itself finished. This happens, Hill argues, when the poet realizes that the poem's form and content are, in T. S. Eliot's phrasing, "finally arranged in the right way."[2] Williams holds that this work of "atoning" is the aim of all true artists. As he sees it, both the necessity which confronts the artist—the deeply felt obligation to be true to what has been given—and the difficulties that arise in the attempt to fulfill that obligation, bear witness to the nature of grace, to its sheer otherness, enormity, and plentitude. And precisely in this witness, the artist and her work, both her work in process and her work as product, reveal something essential about what it means to be human, something which, once realized, is freeing and

ennobling, even as it is also burdening and humbling. And as
with the artist, so with the priest. For Williams, Christian worship is first and last a testimony to the conviction that the life of
faith is not a self-generated, self-sustaining reality. Gathered for
the services of word and sacrament, the believer acknowledges
with the church her existence as "called-out" for community,
summoned to live in a community "created by a communication that must be listened to and answered."[3]

This is the truth of Advent. As George Steiner explains, "the
poet, the composer, the painter," no less than the philosopher and
the mystic, "tell us of the irreducible weight of otherness."[4] And as
a result, in aesthetic experiences, as in religious or mystical ones,
we encounter a reality we know we did not create and cannot
control, a reality that does no violence to us, but "menaces" us
with the call to change.

> The encounter with the aesthetic is together with certain
> modes of religious and of metaphysical experience, the
> most 'ingressive', transformative summons available to
> human experiencing. Again, the shorthand image is that of
> an Annunciation, of "a terrible beauty" or gravity breaking
> into the small house of our cautionary being. If we have
> heard rightly the wing-beat and provocation of that visit,
> the house is no longer habitable in quite the same way as it
> was before. A mastering intrusion has shifted the light (that
> is very precisely, non-mystically, the shift made visible in
> Fra Angelico's *Annunciation*).[5]

"The house is no longer habitable in quite the same way as it was
before." This is the effect of grace's pressure on our lives, a pressure, a "menacing," that is always nudging or jolting us toward
atonement. And it is that grace that we await during Advent.
We learn in this season to dwell in that discomfort, to welcome
the unsettledness it creates, as it prepares us for the "second"
(that is, the next, never final) coming of Christ, a coming which
brings with it exactly what we need to enact the change we feel

called to. For this reason, an aesthetics attuned to the christo-logical reality of Advent teaches us to wait for that which we cannot ourselves bring about.

Awaiting the Terrible Beauty

Accordingly, for Williams, the surest sign of a true "painting" of Christ, whether in art, theology, or lived life, is the discomfort it generates, the sense of tremendous responsibility it imposes, the sense of unimaginable possibility it insinuates. Rightly figured, whether in poetry and fiction or in preaching and pastoral care, Christ unsettles us, and just in that way opens us up to transfig-uration. We can be sure, then, that a work that does not either nudge, prick, or wrench us away from complacency and com-promise, that does not either menace, tease, or woo us toward atonement, simply cannot be true. "When art succeeds, what-ever exactly that means, there has been some opening up to . . . ontological depth. Success is when an artist, in Jacques Maritain's terms, produces an object that has the solidity, the *claritas*, in the medieval sense, the radiance, the luminosity, the density, of real things. The poem, the music, the visual artwork has that den-sity that says that the world is full; the world is not empty; the world is packed . . . 'the world is charged.'"[6]

Gabriel Axel's *Babette's Feast* (1987), the story of a refugee-turned-housekeeper's extravagant gift to an austere Pietist community, unsettles us gently. In the film, which The Criterion Channel describes as "a rousing paean to artistic cre-ation, a delicate evocation of divine grace, and the ultimate film about food," Babette, a French refugee from the Franco-Prussian War, flees from Paris to a tiny village in Denmark, where she agrees to serve for free as a housekeeper for Filippa and Martine, the severe, aging, and unmarried daughters of the pastor who founded the conventicle long before.[7] Each year, a friend from Babette's former life renews her lottery ticket, and after more than a decade, she wins—10,000 francs. Working in secret, she uses the whole of her winnings to throw the most magnificent feast for the sisters and their community. As it comes to them in course upon course of delicacy and succulence, Babette's decadent meal overwhelms the villagers. At first disquieted, then affronted, they soon find themselves enraptured, the bitter differences that had built up over time between them beginning to melt in sweetness. And we find ourselves dizzy with happiness. This just seems *right*.

Ron Hansen's *Mariette in Ecstasy* unsettles us ungently, with something like violence. If *Babette's Feast* is a story of bread and wine, *Mariette* is a story of broken bodies and shed blood. If what Babette did seemed exactly right, what happens to Mariette in Hansen's story, which is "part horror, part suspense,"[8] seems exactly wrong; wrong in precisely the right way. Hansen's story is also sexually charged: when we first meet Mariette, before she joins the Sisters of the Crucifixion, she "esteems her breasts as she has seen men esteem them" and "haunts her milk-white skin with her hands," praying, "Even this I give You."[9] On Christmas, the young postulant receives the stigmata, or so she claims. But her wounds, and her words about her wounds, fracture her community. In the words of the Mother Superior:

> I have been troubled by God's motives for this. I see no reasons for it. Is it so Mariette Baptiste will be praised and esteemed by the pious? Or is it so she shall be humiliated and jeered at by skeptics? Is it to honor religion and humble science? What are these horrible wounds, really? A trick of anatomy, a bleeding challenge to medical diagnosis, a brief and baffling injury that hasn't yet, in six hundred years, changed our theology or our religious practices? Have you any idea how disruptive you've been? You are awakening hollow talk and half-formed opinions that have no place in our priory, and I have no idea why God would be doing this. To you.[10]

On the one hand, Babette represents something of the loveliness of Jesus' character—his allure, his charm. Mariette, on the other hand, represents the scandal of his sufferings and the even greater scandal of his intimacy with God in his suffering. But each in her own way figures Christ, so that we feel the pressure of otherness, whether heavy or light, constant or sudden. Does the same hold true for painting? I would argue that it does. Rembrandt's *Head of Christ*, for example, has something of the same warm and worn humanity I find in Stéphane Audran's Babette. And Hans Holbein the Younger's *Dead Christ* disturbs me in much the same way *Mariette in Ecstasy* does. One painting beautifully evokes Jesus' gentleness. The other forces us to face the ugly truth of his tragic, torturous death, and the irrevocable fact of his being dead. But both "work" precisely in that they suggest a "how much more," which cannot be taken in all at once.

If, as I have been arguing, artistic representations of Christ are true just in that they are troubling and impenetrable, baffling and evocative, then Axel's Babette and Hansen's Mariette, as well as Rembrandt's and Holbein's paintings, succeed as figurations of Christ in ways Malick's Franz Jägerstätter does not. Malick's saint's story is inspirational. But it does not quite intimate mystery or arouse us entirely away from ourselves "to the wonder." Jägerstätter is perhaps more a memorialized Christ figure than a sacramental or iconic one. He indicates, more than incites. And so, while his story, and the film that tells it, are beautiful in a number of ways, and while they remind us of so much that is terrible, they never quite radiate the "terrible beauty" that makes our hope something other than wishfulness.

Malick paints his true Christ in *The Thin Red Line* (1998). In Jim Caviezel's breathtaking performance, Pvt. Witt bodies forth an enigmatic innocence and calm, a purity of spirit touched with a sublime, unfathomable sadness. At the story's beginning, Witt is AWOL on a Pacific island, living with the Melanesian Christians, working with them, playing with their children. Just before he is captured and returned to his company, he stands on the beach transfixed by the villagers' joyous, processional rendition of a pidgin hymn, "Jisas, Yu Holem Hand Blong Mi," which praises Christ for finding "every good thing in this world." Unlike anyone else in Charlie Company, Witt looks for the good things, and finds them, even amidst the horrors of the war. Like Steinbeck's Jim Casy, he wonders at the oneness of humanity, "each like a coal drawn from the fire." "We were a family. How did it break up and come apart? So that now we're turned against each other. Each standing in the other's light. How did we lose the good that was given us? Let it slip away? Scatter it careless? What's keeping us from reaching out? Touching the glory?"

One evening, after the first day of the battle, Witt and the skeptical, weary Sgt. Welsh (played without sneering or self-importance by Sean Penn) find themselves together, and the older man questions the younger, trying to sound his depths: "I feel sorry for you, kid. This Army's gonna kill you. What difference do you think you can make, one single man in all this madness? If you die, it's gonna be for nothing." Witt gazes back at Welsh, his eyes shimmering with tears, and says nothing, only glancing up at the moon. Later, in an abandoned hut in the early morning, Welsh sounds Witt again: "Why are you such a troublemaker, Witt? Still believing the beautiful light, are you? How do you do that? You're a magician to me." Witt responds with an unconditional calm: "I still see a spark in you," he says. After Witt is killed, and buried, Welsh grieves over his grave. "Where's your spark now?" Then, as the company assembles and moves out, the sergeant's voice is heard in prayer as voice-over: "If I never meet you in this life, let me feel the lack. A glance from your eyes, and my life would be yours." Welsh can pray this prayer just because it has already been answered. He feels the lack, and in that feeling, feels the weight of an infinite plentitude. He is already seen, already claimed. In the beginning, Witt is found by the Christ who finds all the good in the world. And in the end, having found and lost Witt, Welsh asks to find and be found, as well.

All to say, Caviezel's Witt is true in ways his Jesus in Mel Gibson's *The Passion of the Christ* is not. And Malick's and Caviezel's Witt is true in ways that Malick's and Diehl's Jägerstätter is not. Why? What makes the difference? Just this: Witt lives and dies in relation to a reality not of his own making, a reality that grasps, but is not grasped. He abides in his soul—that is, in God—and so he shines, as all things do in the vision of God. Caviezel's Jesus is a cipher, a symbol. But Caviezel's Witt is redolently himself, and he is glorious, which is why we feel the weight of his presence, his bearing, his words, his silence, his gaze, his tears, his death. And this, whatever one might call it, is what makes the difference not only between true and false Christ figures (like Gibson's Jesus), but also between true and merely "factual" ones (like Malick's Jägerstätter).

But this does not at all mean that *A Hidden Life* is false or worthless. It is, as I have just suggested, "factual," in much the same way that Malick's first film, *Badlands*, is "factual." As Matt Zoller Seitz explains, Malick's debut "has a lyrical style, but a detached point of view. It is at once a clinical case-study of deeply amoral people, and a fairytale about a boy and a girl who are young, dumb, and in love . . . The case study aspect of this film is chilling, and Malick captures it with almost scientific exactness. Holly and Kit just aren't wired right."[11] *A Hidden Life* is also lyrical, and detached. It is also a case study, although this time the subjects, Franz and Fani, are deeply moral persons. And it is also a fairy tale, which ends in death, albeit this time with martyrdom, not murder. If *Badlands* is a documentation of the mystery of iniquity, *A Hidden Life* is a documentation of the mystery of faith. And even if it is not glorious, it reminds us that the glorious can and does happen, and indeed has happened in our world. And it reminds us that painting a true Christ matters only if there is a true Christ who makes the painting worthwhile. Christ is the truth, and he makes us true. Only if we do not forget this, can we know why it is important, and possible, to represent in our art him and ourselves and his world, which he has entrusted to us. Seen this way, Malick's *A Hidden Life* is self-effacing, not artless; an act of restraint and discretion; and a reminder that the experience of the glorious is not any more inherently sanctifying than is the experience of the common. And the truth is, we need both

A Hidden Life, and its facticity, as well as *The Thin Red Line*, and its truthfulness. We need both indication and provocation, both commonness and glory, both memorials and sacraments. And we need them because our lives are meant to be lived both in facticity and truthfulness, imminence and transcendence, until we can see the transcendence of the fact and the imminence of the true. This is what we must come to believe if what we confess in the creed about Christ is true. In Advent, we are called to attend to this confession and to its Christ.

The Powerlessness and the Glory

In the light of all we have said, then, we can see that Christ figures may be true in one way or another, either glorious or not, without being false. And the same holds for all artistic representation, whether made by Christians or not, and whether they take Christ as their subject or not. Not surprisingly, if, as we confess, Jesus of Nazareth is the Word through whom and in whom all things are made; if he is the truth that makes whatever is true, true; the purity that makes whatever is pure, pure; and the beauty that makes whatever is beautiful, lovely. Any truthful, pure, or beautiful representation, no matter its subject, no matter its form, necessarily bears something of the weight of his glory, because it is his glory that gives them their being. Sometimes, as in *A Hidden Life*, that glory is veiled, as it was in the "hidden years" of Jesus' own life. Other times, it shines forth, as it does in his birth and his baptism, his ministry and his death, his resurrection and his ascension. But it is always there, whether we experience it or not, and whether we know we have experienced it or not.

Makoto Fujimura tells the story of his conversion as the working out of a convergence of experiences during his time studying Nihonga, an ancient, extravagant style of Japanese painting, in a doctoral program in Tokyo. He had recently encountered Georges Rouault's Passion paintings in a visit to Tokyo's Idemitsu Museum, and their "terribly beauty" moved him in ways he hardly sensed at first. One day, as he was working in his studio, a professor entered unannounced, interrupting him, and the professor was thrown back by what he saw: "Mako, that surface is so beautiful, it's terrifying." Fujimura instinctively destroyed the painting, realizing, without understanding, that he could not live with such a beauty. Soon, he encountered it again in the Jesus who speaks from the cross in William Blake's "Jerusalem," and this time, he was claimed by it—although, again, he did not know for a long time what exactly he had decided in that moment.[12]

Fujimura's story brings us up hard against a paradox. In fiction and film, as well as in painting, some of the truest representations of Christ, the ones which in the Spirit present to us the truth of who we are and how we are loved, are in crucial respects deeply untrue. Besides Blake's Jesus or Rouault's Christs, consider, for example, the whiskey priest in Graham Greene's *The Power and the Glory*. Is he a Christ figure? Yes, but an admittedly sketchy one, one that gives only the barest outline, the slightest, merely suggestive, resemblance. There is a "grotesque disproportion between figure and model."[13] Still, the figure does look like the model in one respect: constrained by compassion, he loves until the end, refusing to save himself and leave others alone in their doom. In spite of his character, in spite of his lack of faith, the pattern of his life takes "the attitude of the cross."[14] Against all expectation, it is precisely the emptiness within the sketched outline that gives this figure life, suggesting that Christ is everything the priest is not. Like the troubled monk in Frederick Buechner's *Godric*, Greene's priest is both like Christ and unlike him, but it is the unlikeness that makes the likeness compelling.

On the morning of his death, the nameless priest awakes at dawn "with a huge feeling of hope which suddenly and completely left him." He tries, and fails, to remember the Act of Contrition, and catching sight of his own shadow, curses himself for having been so foolish as to stay when others fled. "What an impossible fellow I am, he thought, and how useless. I have done nothing for anybody."

He felt only an immense disappointment because he had to go to God empty-handed, with nothing done at all. It seemed to him, at that moment, that it would have been quite easy to have been a saint. It would only have needed a little self-restraint and a little courage. He felt like someone who has missed happiness by seconds at an appointed place. He knew now that at the end there was only one thing that counted—to be a saint.[15]

In truth, this priest, sordid and squalid as he is, dies as a martyr. And in the book's final chapter, a mother rebukes her children for talking about the priest's "funny smell": "You must never say that again. He may be one of the saints."[16] And he *is* saintly, but only because he learned how to live with his sinfulness. The whiskey priest is a figure of Christ precisely because he knew he could not change his own disfigurement. He knew he could not heal himself. As he himself says, "Oh yes, I believe [in the forgiveness of sins] . . . But I can't absolve myself."[17]

But if this paradox is true of artistic representation, then it must reveal something about Christ himself, as well, for he is the art that makes all art artful.[18] Jesus is God, and with God (John 1:1-2); infinite, and finite; fully divine, and fully human; creator, and creature; unbegotten, and begotten; the "image of the invisible God," and "the firstborn of all creation" (Col 1:15), "the reflection of God's glory and the exact imprint of God's very being" (Heb 1:3); worshipped, and worshipful; obeyed, and obedient; model, and figure; truth, and fact; presentation, and representation. Precisely so, he bodies forth infinitely the truth of God and in that embodiment, indwells all finite things as their truth. And that, in turn, means that all things "shine," all things smell of infinity. As Rahner says, "all beings are by their nature symbolic, because they necessarily 'express' themselves in order to attain their own true nature."[19] And we might add that as they present themselves in expression, they are presented to us for our work of representation, by which we present ourselves to God and find how he is present to us.

Ascending and Descending

This is true not only of "nature," but also of art. Jesus says to Nicodemus: "*Just as* Moses lifted up the serpent in the wilderness, *so must* the Son of Man be lifted up" (John 3:14). Obviously, he is referring to the story of the brazen serpent, the figure Moses made and exhibited, which healed the Israelites who looked to it (Num 21:9). But why does Jesus say his "lifting up" *must* happen *just as* the serpent's did? Because there exists an inner reciprocity, an asymmetrical but equalizing exchange, between the Word, without whom not one thing came into being, and everything we make or have made. In other words, whatever we make, however we make it, turns out to be more and other than what we intended. And whatever we make, however we make it, turns out to be apt for representing Christ. Our creativity, our artistic mastery, cannot fail to witness to our createdness, and so to the creator and his artistry.

"If I have told you about earthly things and you do not believe, how can you believe if I tell you about heavenly things? No one has ascended into heaven except the one who descended from heaven, the Son of Man" (John 3:12-13). In this, Jesus reveals that the "earthly" is joined to the "heavenly" by a ladder of signification and representation, a ladder which leads "up" and "down," not from the finite to the infinite, but from the finite to the infinitized infinitizing, and back again. He, "the Son of Man," made this ladder in his ascending—that is, his death—and his descending—that is, his birth. And in this way, he created all things with a capacity for "movement," a capacity for exchange, transposition, communion. We cannot believe the heavenly if we do not know the earthly; hence, as Rahner says, poetry is necessary. Without it we will not know how to allow words, including the words of the gospel, the words of the Scripture, and the words of the liturgy, which are of course authoritative in a way other words are not, to call "us out of the little house of our homely, close-hugged truths into the strangeness of the night that is our real home . . ."[20]

What Rahner says of poetry is true of all art. The truth is, Malick's painter painted not because he needed to make a living, but because painting made it possible for him to live. It was necessary for him, as it is for us, because without it he could not be himself, could not know how he was known. He rightly longed to paint a true Christ, rightly lamented the "comfortable" images that obscure rather than illuminate reality. But he was wrong to imagine that if he could only screw up the courage to suffer greatly, he would somehow become capable of making great things. The good and bad news is, we are always capable of painting a true Christ. And it is only our diseased fantasies of self-determination in freedom from God and neighbor that make us forget that capability.

This is why we are forbidden to make "any graven image, or any likeness." A strange prohibition, given that because the God who made us is the God he is, we are bound to create. Like it or not, we cannot *not* grave images and likenesses. So why forbid it? Because in our fallenness, God must teach us how not to disfigure what he has made for us, or what we make for him. As John of Damascus discerned, despite his anti-Semitism, this commandment must be understood not in its "letter," but by its "spirit."[21] So understood, it comes clear that the commandment was given to us so we would know how "to avoid superstitious error, to be with God in the knowledge of the truth, to worship God alone, to enjoy the fulness of his knowledge."[22] The prohibition against idols protects not God's reputation, but the integrity of our creativity and artistic representation. And because idolatry consists in perception and apperception, not in reality—as St. Paul says, "an idol is nothing" (1 Cor 8:4 AKJV)—John assures us that if our mind is habituated to God's in Christ, we are freed from idolatry, delivered both from the fear that everything depends on what we can make and from the fear that what we have disfigured reveals the deepest truth of our nature.[23] If our mind is habituated to God's, we know that idols are nothing but as-yet-unrecognized icons. And we see everything in God and God in Christ and Christ in everything.

Advent teaches us that this is what we long for in all of our longings. We long for God and for ourselves, for atonement, for Christ, the Christ of the ladder, the one who teaches us how to descend and ascend, how to make and how not to make, how to say what must be heard and hear what cannot be said. We long to follow and not merely to admire. We long to feel the lack, and to meet the demand. We long both to paint a true Christ, and even more for the true Christ to paint us, not comfortable and haloed, but suffering, as we stir from dreaming. We long for the warmth and the light; to touch the glory, and to be touched by it. We long to see all things shining.

2

All Things Beautiful in His Time

Christmas

The Time Being is the most trying time of all.
W. H. Auden

But when the fullness of time had come, God sent his Son, born of a woman.
Galatians 4:4 (NABRE)

She bore no more than other women bore, but in her belly's globe that desert night the earth's full burden swayed.
Mary Karr

Sculpting in Time

Christians are "the most sublime materialists."[1] And they are the most sublime chronologists, as well, and for the same reason: at Christmas each year, we celebrate the coming of God, a coming which happened, we confess, both "in the flesh" and "in the fullness of time." We celebrate Christmas, both because we believe God reveals himself fully in the one who is born, and because we believe the one who is born bears within himself the whole truth and nothing but the truth about us and about all that exists. Christmas, in other words, is not for us merely something that happened once upon a time. It is *the* happening, an event that already always has happened to all other events, storying them as God's. Thus, as we are striving, mostly subconsciously and in dreams, to reconcile our memories, our decisions, and our hopes, we remain confident that time is God's and therefore good for us, even in its fallenness.[2] We can trust this because we trust him and what he accomplished in the womb of Mary and in her love for her son. Loving him, she loved in one act both her God and her neighbor as herself—an act uniquely possible for a mother whose child is God. And at Christmas, in her, in the son she loved, creator and creation, eternity and time, infinity and finitude were knit together so tightly that even death could not undo the knot.

Christian Wiman has said "art is so often better at theology than theology is," because it is more willing to face the silence and the "unmeaning"—those aspects of God and our own existence that simply lie beyond our reach, ungraspable and unmasterable.[3] That kind of courage is sorely needed, given that our theologies of time, to say nothing of our celebrations of Christmas, are almost invariably superficial and sentimental. Robert Jenson's theology stands out as a much-needed exception, and it is exceptional precisely because he appreciates the relationship between time and beauty, contending that time is what it is, and beauty is what it is, because God is the triune God he is. For Jenson, God's life is dramatic and coherent, like a drama, with a beginning and a meaningful, and meaningfully surprising, end, which is why creation makes a history and not merely a cosmos. "Religion" names the attempt to escape temporality, to protect ourselves from the past or the future by some means, liturgical, moral, or theurgic. But the gospel tells another story: creation is nothing but the time God has made for us, and salvation is his work of harmonizing past and present and future, and drawing us into the rhythms of his own life; just so, "the end is music."[4]

Theologians should be the first to see our need for the arts, and for what they alone can teach us about what time is and how we are to live it. To state the obvious, different arts do this differently, both in form and in content, and often in ways the artist did not intend. A sculpture, for example, like a painting, like a photograph, can be taken in almost at once, whereas a novel, like a poem or a song, takes time. And Klee's *Angelus Novus* was not intended as a comment on time, but Benjamin was not wrong to see it as the angel of history, blown into the future by the force of "progress," looking back in horror at the piling debris. In the same way, David Jones' long poem, *Anathemata*, is not strictly about time, but it nonetheless forces on us a sense of time's almost limitless breadths and depths, while leaving us feeling that somehow, all these times, historic and prehistoric, and all that has happened, is happening, or will happen in them, cohere like a voyage, like a sacrifice.

Film is a unique art, and, if Tarkovsky is right, this is precisely because of the way it captures and releases time. In his view, the virtue of cinema is its power to "appropriate time," "to record time in outward and visible signs, recognizable to the feelings," capturing the "very movement of reality" in images that create "the illusion of the infinite," allowing the absolute, the transcendent, to "make itself felt."[5] And he does not merely suggest that this might be so; he attempts to explain how it works. In his method, the director films an event, like a kiss or a leap from a bridge, or an object, like a cup or a stone; and in that filming, catches patterns of time, which are inherent in the fact that has been filmed. If a film is to consist of more than one shot, then those shots must be edited, of course; and at that point, according to Tarkovsky, the director's responsibility is to recognize the "time-truth" and "time-pressure" already existing in the images.[6] Hence, the director's primary task is to find in her edits the best ways to honor those pressures, that truth. In a word, editing is investigative, not creative. "Editing does not engender, or recreate, a new quality; it brings out a quality already inherent in the frames that it joins." If this is done rightly, then "the unified, living structure inherent in the film" manifests as a new, transfiguring reality.[7]

The Wonder, the Knight, the Song, and the Tree

As I said in the previous chapter, at least some of Malick's films are influenced by Tarkovsky's work, if not also his philosophy of cinema. And his films, like Tarkovsky's, take time, creating the possibility for us to see what time makes of us and what we make of it. He prefers long, lingering takes, as Tarkovsky did, and some of his shots quote Tarkovsky; think, for example, of grass waving under water in *The Tree of Life* (2011), which calls back scenes at the beginning and end of *Solaris* (1972), or Mrs. O'Brien's levitation, which recalls the intertwined rising of Alexander and Maria in *The Sacrifice* (1986). But the comparisons run deeper than stylistic or thematic similarities. Malick's films, like Tarkovsky's, do not merely provoke philosophical reflection; they are themselves works of philosophy, born of the conviction that the eternal is not above or outside temporality, but *in* it, in the experience of it, the experience which opens us up to the absolute. To quote Tarkovsky again, "The allotted function of art is not, as is often assumed, to put across ideas, to propagate thoughts, to serve as an example. The aim of art is to prepare a person for death, to plough and harrow his soul, rendering it capable of turning to good."[8]

Stanley Cavell considered Malick's first two films—*Badlands* (1973) and *Days of Heaven* (1978)—"Heideggerian cinema." But beginning with *The Thin Red Line* (1998), Malick's work, without becoming less philosophical, has become more and more theological. And his masterpiece, *Tree of Life*, and the films that have followed it, are perhaps better called Augustinian cinema. These films are concerned with the relation of nature and grace, time and eternity, but even more than that, they are meant to body forth the glory of a life lived toward God. In this way, Malick is unlike Tarkovsky: his films are "not vaguely or ambivalently religious or spiritual but . . . distinctly and explicitly Christian." Indeed, it is not too much to call them "evangelical": "they function as cinematic 'liturgies' that seek to orient the hearts and minds of viewers toward the Christian story—a way of seeing and interacting with God and the world—helping us . . . recover the good within us and reach out to touch the glory."[9]

Gregory of Nyssa suggests that the spiritual life follows a journey mapped by the differences between Proverbs, Ecclesiastes, and Song of Songs. The arc of the maturing Christian life moves from the first to the latter, much as Israel moved from Egypt, the land of their captivity, through the wilderness, to Canaan, the land of promise. Proverbs "exercises soul so that it can desire not corporeal things but virtue," and Ecclesiastes, in turn, "trains desire to long for what is beyond appearance, beyond the grasp of senses." Song of Songs, at last, leads soul into the luminous dark of pure intimacy with the God who is above all names, so that image and imagelessness, passion and dispassion are reconciled and surpassed, transposed into divinity.[10] Without exaggerating the comparisons, it seems that something like this same trajectory shapes Malick's later work, as well, beginning with *Tree of Life* and continuing through *To the Wonder*, *Knight of Cups*, and *Song to Song*.[11] But in Malick's Augustinian vision, the journey to God is also the turn, or, better, return to oneself. Moving inward, the pilgrim is led first all the way down, into the depths of memory, the seat of human self-transcendence, and then outward and upward, toward the God beyond who is found in the end to be all in all: within and without, beneath and beside and above.[12]

At the beginning of his *Confessions*, Augustine knows that God has made us for himself, so he knows that we must be restless until we find our rest in God. Toward the end, he has learned that the God we seek without, among the things that exist, is and has always been within us, as the center and ground of our being. Realizing this, we recognize with him that we cannot be reconciled to ourselves without first being reconciled to God. We recognize, again, as he did, that we have not and could not have made ourselves, and that we also cannot make ourselves happy. To "return to God" is actually the only way in which a created thing can "return to itself."[13]

Augustine experiences time as a threat, a force of estrangement, and then, in prayer, begs God to save him from that estrangement. As he prays, he realizes that memory points the way toward God, because it allows us to relate to ourselves and thus to see that we did not make ourselves any more than we made or could have made God or the world. "The absolute future turns out to be the ultimate past and the way to reach it is through remembrance. By recalling a past that is prior to all possibilities of earthly, mundane experience, man who was created and did not make himself finds the utmost limit of his own past—his own 'whence.'"[14]

All of this is felt with force in Malick's later cinema, and in *The Tree of Life* it is expressed as a theodicy or anti-theodicy. We should not miss the fact that the film opens with lines from the book of Job: "Where were you when I laid the foundation of the earth? . . . When the morning stars sang together, and all the sons of God shouted for joy?" (Job 38:4, 7). Or the fact that it is told as a prayer of complaint and petition and praise, which we overhear and oversee. What we overhear and oversee is the story of Jack O'Brien, a high-achieving, middle-aged architect in the American Southwest, returning at last to God and to himself, a returning that unfolds over the course of a single day, the anniversary of Jack's brother's death. Near the beginning of the film, Jack is at home, early in the morning, and we hear in whispered voiceovers his unspoken, perhaps even unthought, prayers: "How did you come to me? In what shape? What disguise?" He lights a candle in his brother's memory, its votive flame dancing like the divine light, which is the film's first and last image. As the flame shudders, we hear the beginning of Jack's confessions: "I see the child I was. I see my brother. True. Kind. He died when he was nineteen." Then, we follow him as he arrives at his high-rise office, hear him as he calls to apologize to his father for what he had said, see him slumped in his chair near the window, wandering in the caves of his memories. In his mind's eye, he sees his brother on a beach, and hears his call: "Find me." The rest of the film tells the story of that seeking and finding.[15]

At first, Jack sees himself as an adult, standing near his grieving parents, observing their grief, in shots recalling scenes from Tarkovsky's *Sacrifice*. Then, we see the twirling divine light again, and hear his mother's prayer, which he now makes his own:

"Lord, why? Where were you? Did you know? Who are we to you? Answer me. We cry to you. My soul, my son. Hear us. Life of my life, I search for you, my hope, my child." Her questions hang over the long creation montage that follows, a cinematic *représentation* of God's speech to Job out of the whirlwind: primordial blackness, fields of fire, the rupture of stars, gleaming horizons, falling waterfalls and rising canyons, swells of smoke and ash, blood curling in the water, a frenzy of sharks, a plesiosaur, a gaping wound in its side, dying on the beach, the same beach on which his brother, R. L., is standing when he calls to Jack, a plummeting asteroid, the doom of the dinosaurs, breaking waves . . . And then a bell tolls, and Jack recovers his own voice: "You spoke to me through her."

Jack's mother, like Augustine's, intercedes for him, and her prayers, like Monica's, are heard. He begins his search, taking the same path Augustine had taken, out toward nature: "You spoke with me from the sky, the trees, before I knew I loved you, believed in you." In the end, Jack finds his brother, but only by first finding himself in his own memories. Following the guide, he is led through a door, the door named in the first lines of his confession, into a wasteland. There, he sees his younger self running ahead and over a rise. He follows, and we see flashes of the Big Bang: a new creation has begun. He is led to the beach, the beach where the plesiosaur died, and his brothers, his mother, his father, and neighbors welcome him, all appearing exactly as they did when he was twelve—the moment he was estranged from himself. He moves along the beach with them, resting his hand on his father's shoulder, much as his father had done to him so often when he was a boy. At last, we are led again to a door, and Jack sees himself and his mother as she makes her prayer of release: "I give him to you. I give you my son," she breathes, lifting her arms, opening her hands. The "Amen" is sung, and we see Jack coming down the elevator of his office building. Outside, he twirls, just like his mother had done, just as the divine light does, and he smiles, only slightly.

Many critics and reviewers of the film misread this final scene on the beach as happening in heaven. Roger Ebert, for example, describes it as "a vision of an afterlife, a desolate landscape on which quiet people solemnly recognize and greet one another, and all is understood in the fullness of time." But what Malick gives is a vision of Jack's recollection: his return to himself, his return to God.[16] "Jack's memories are healed by penetrating back to the beginning of all beginnings, and when they are joined with hope for the end beyond all endings."[17] But Jack's only access to this beginning of all beginnings is through imitating his mother's graceful surrender, her offering up of her lost son to God in prayer. Releasing his brother, releasing his mother, releasing himself—these all happen at once for Jack, and so he becomes like his mother, like his brother, like himself—and so is bound to God. They have led him to God's door.

Something much like this happens at the end of *The New World*, too. Pocahontas, at last, reconciles herself to the Old World, her strange new world, having received and chosen the grace of her husband. Playing hide-and-seek with her son, she asks, laughing, "Thomas, where are you?"—a seemingly throwaway line, easily missed, but in fact it subtly draws together the stories of Adam and Eve, whom God seeks, and the story of Thomas, who seeks God, into Pocahontas' story, suggesting that all seeking is one in the end. The next moment, we hear her last words, whispered in voice-over: "Mother, now I know where you live." After she dies, she returns to nature, as Jack did in *The Tree of Life*, as Maria did in *To the Wonder*, dancing and delighted. Hence, at the risk of putting it all a bit too nicely, we might say that while it is true that not all who wander are lost, it is also true that only those who wonder are found. We wander until we wonder. And then our journey begins.

The End of Time

As Cavell said, Malick's cinema casts a full-bodied theology of time. This is why his stories are unconventionally told: not in an attempt to be "poetic," but in the effort to be true to our actual experience. They show that we do not experience time as such, but *times*—high and low, slow and fast. And they show how these times break us or bind us. In classical Greek, the word for beauty is derived from the word for hour. And in English, too, we talk about having a lovely time, about beautiful timing, about appropriate or opportune times. Usually, however, time in our experience is anything but beautiful. In myriad ways, temporality estranges us from ourselves, making it so that we are either caught up in the past or consumed by the present or fixated on the future, incapable of being fully present in the moment in the ways we truly want to be, in our heart of hearts, and in the ways others need us to be. This is why Rick laments in *Knight of Cups*, "I wonder where I was in all that time." When time and the beautiful are misaligned, when our times are out of rhythm with God's time, desire is enflamed. And because we are not yet reconciled to ourselves, we invariably seek to fulfill those desires in all the wrong ways: "To Carthage then I came / burning burning burning burning."[18] Sometimes, however, in Malick's films, as in "real life," time and beauty do align, like lovers; they con-spire, breathe together, making love. When they do, our longing for the infinite is fulfilled, without in any sense being quenched, and out of this fulfillment mercy is born, and every other kindness.

For Malick, as for Augustine, time cannot end except in fulfillment, and time is fulfilled only as love reaches its fullness, and love reaches its fullness only through surrender to the infinite. In *The Tree of Life*, Jack's mother tells her boys, "The only way to be happy is to love. Unless you love, your life will flash by." Remembering her words brings Jack to the door that leads to his brother, and standing at the door, and passing through it, he prays: "Brother. Keep us. Guide us. To the end of time." And that end comes as he, with his mother, gives up his brother, her son, to God, a surrender which not only changes his present and his future, but at the same time also changes his past. This is what marks it as an encounter with the eternal, with the goodness that makes what time has done to us and what we have done with our time worthwhile in spite of everything. Hence, as Malick sees, standing in Augustine's light, the migration to God begins in making peace with finitude, in reconciliation to the mysterious incomprehensibility of our own existence. In that sense, Christmas comes after, not before, Good Friday.

Perhaps this is why, in Malick's vision, the arc of spiritual maturation begins, not in Proverbs, but in Job, in the confrontation with the God who seems so indifferent to our suffering, if not also the cause of it. But Malick hears in God's question not a rebuke, but an invitation, a summons. For him, "Where were you when I laid the foundations of the earth?" is not a censure, but a clue, an intimation. If Job tries to answer the question that has been asked of him, and keeps trying, he will find eventually not only God but also himself. And if he finds himself, his story will change. Of course, as I will explore in a later chapter, Job succumbs too quickly, gives up the fight, represses his anger and his fear, and so misses his moment. But Christ does not. In Gethsemane, he confronts the whirlwind, showing that God is not simply a name for what we cannot comprehend, and that the Yes of faith cannot be spoken until the Nevertheless of personhood and self-preservation is spoken. But he does more than show the way: he creates it. In his self-possessed yielding, he makes it so we can speak against the dying of the light, but without rage, and can go gently into that good night because we know the one who waits in it is himself gentle.

We should not pretend that we are not afraid of death, even the little deaths that happen to us all of the time. It is true, of course, that time makes it possible for us to grow, to mature; but it is also true that time forces us into loss, separating us from ourselves and from those whom we love. We say time is a healer, but it is perhaps truer to say it is steward, a warden, not healing our wounds but only distancing us from the events of our wounding, as well as those who have wounded us—including our past selves. Even Jesus, God-in-time, experienced this loss, this distancing.

As Donald MacKinnon says, "For Christ there is the estrangement involved in abandoning his human origins, in tearing his
life up by the roots to put himself at the disposal of the men and
the women to whom he believed himself sent. The marks of that
estrangement are upon him, reflected in the harshness of his
rebuffs to his mother, and to his brothers."[19] In spite of this, however, there was for Christ no loss of compassion, no bitterness
for past hurts, no sorrow for a lost future. Why? Because he lived
open to eternity, and thus reconciled to his past and to his future.
In the language of John's Gospel, he lived every moment in the
light of his "hour," which was always "to come" and already "at
hand." Those who joined him in that hour found their own freedom, as well. At the end of the Gospel, as he is dying, Jesus sees
his mother and the beloved disciple at the foot of his cross, and he
gives them to each other, so that they become to each other what
he had been to them: "Mother, behold your son; son, behold your
mother." The Gospel says "*from that hour* the disciple took her
into his own home" (John 19:27), and that in that moment "Jesus
knew that all now was finished" (John 19:28).

Again and again in John's Gospel, this "hour" has been antic-
ipated. At the wedding in Cana, Jesus tells his mother, "My hour
has not yet come" (John 2:4). He tells the Samaritan woman at the
well, "the hour is coming, and is now here" (John 4:23). He says
it again, after he heals the paralyzed man by the pool on the Sab-
bath: "The hour is coming, and is now here, when the dead will
hear the voice of the Son of God, and those who hear will live"
(John 5:25). His enemies try to arrest him, or to kill him, but fail,
"because his hour had not yet come" (John 7:30; 8:20). Finally, the
moment does come, and he does not shy away from it, although
he feels its weight:

> "The hour has come for the Son of Man to be glorified. Very
> truly, I tell you, unless a grain of wheat falls into the earth
> and dies, it remains just a single grain; but if it dies, it bears
> much fruit. Those who love their life lose it, and those who
> hate their life in this world will keep it for eternal life . . .

Now my soul is troubled. And what should I say—'Father, save me from this hour'? No, it is for this reason that I have come to this hour." (John 12:23-27)

Obviously, this seems to run against the grain of the other Gospels and their stories of Jesus' agony in Gethsemane. But there is no contradiction. In those stories, we hear him give voice to the naturally human fear of death, the fear of the unknown, the fear of the uncontrollable. In John's Gospel, he voices the naturally divine determination to overcome those fears in our stead and on our behalf. And Christians confess that in him, personally, these two natural responses are aligned, so that his fears reveal that the Father does not desire our death any more than he desires his own, and his obedience in spite of his fears reveals that the Father will not let even death separate us from him or from one another. The Spirit of God is the Spirit of life; therefore, Christ's desire to live is good and revelatory. And his willingness nonetheless to obey the Father and to love us "to the end," even if that requires him to suffer the humiliation of a criminal's death among criminals, is also good. All to say, both his fears and his resolve witness to the same reality, which Rahner calls "the blessed secret of Christmas": divinity and humanity "arise from one and the same common ground"—the heart of the Father, who begets the Son and creates all things in and through and for him, who gives up the Son for the sake of all things, but does not forsake him, raising him up from the dead and all creation with him. Consequently, the secret of being human and the secret of being God are one secret, and we can therefore face our fears without fear, knowing that our finitude is bounded by his infinity, and knowing the fact that we are incomprehensible to ourselves is nothing but a witness to the unimaginable and inexhaustible goodness of God toward us.[20] In spite of everything, and without ignoring anything, we can live at peace with temporality, striving to love as we have been loved, pondering in our hearts the mystery of his life, which ends, as ours must, in death, confident that all things, past, future, or present, can be made beautiful because time is Christ's and we are Christ's and Christ is God's.

And this is no less true for those who no longer hold their own memories, and for those whose most formative memories are traumatic. If, as we confess, in Christ the infinite and the finite are knit together, then he alone can hold all things together (Col 1:17)—and does. And since that is true, we can dare to face the truth, however ugly, however dark, about ourselves, about the world. And since that is true, we can dare to come apart, if we need to, and let things fall apart, if they must. Following Jesus, as Auden says we should, through the land of unlikeness and the kingdom of anxiety,[21] we find we are kept in company with those who are at a loss, those who are losing, those who have been lost. And just so, we know the test of a work of art—or a theology—is in its success or failure to bring some measure of healing to them,[22] and in its success or failure to wound us in ways that awaken mercy for them and for ourselves. And in that mercy, given and received, we find we can at last take Christmas seriously, find we are ready at last to consider it as "more than an agreeable possibility," as the blessing that runs "far as the curse is found," and so much farther still, "remembering the stable where for once in our lives, everything became a You and nothing was an It."[23]

3

The Name above All Names

Epiphany

The essential American soul is hard, isolate, stoic, and a killer.
It has never yet melted.

D. H. Lawrence

Acquire the Spirit of Peace and a thousand souls around you
will be saved.

St. Seraphim of Sarov

Tell me, I pray thee, thy name.

Genesis 32:29 AKJV

The Western Stars

In a wide-ranging and widely praised trilogy, Richard Slotkin has explored the lengths and breadths of what he calls the myth of the American frontier, seeking both to make sense of how it developed and to explain why it continues to work so powerfully in the popular imagination. The first volume, *Regeneration through Violence*, traced the shape of cultural narratives from the founding of Jamestown to the beginning of the Civil War. In deep detail, Slotkin shows how leading American writers worked out an image of the representative American—in contrast with Europeans on the one hand and the Native Americans on the other. What emerged was a symbolic figure, the "hunter-hero," and stories of his adventures in "the savage new world." John Filson's Daniel Boone was

the first archetype: noble, yet down-to-earth; fearless, yet pragmatic; predisposed to peace, but ready to commit unspeakable violence if necessary; living out a representational story of
exploration and conquest. In the tale of Boone's exploits, published in 1784 as an appendix to his book on the "discovery" and
"settlement" of Kentucky, Filson found a way to weave together
"the historical mission of the American people, and the destiny
appointed for the wilderness by natural law and divine Providence."[1] And over time, his Boone narrative emerged, in Slotkin's
words, as "the first nationally viable statement of a myth of the
frontier," providing colonists with assurance they were called to
possess the land and that their struggles were divinely ordered.
In other words, according to this new frontier mythology, indi-
vidual and national self-realization and self-transcendence were
understood to be achieved through conflict; therefore, the "new
world" had to be both God-given and godforsaken. Only through
the heroic acts of those who had forsaken the luxuries of civilization and ventured out into the wilds to face merciless enemies,
both without and within, at last taking dominion over the land,
could America fulfill her exceptional calling and achieve her
predestined salvation—not only for herself but also for others,
including those whom she has conquered.

In the trilogy's final volume, *Gunfighter Nation*, published
almost twenty years after *Regeneration*, Slotkin considers the
import of John F. Kennedy's "New Frontier" presidential cam-
paign slogan and his request for Robert Frost's "The Gift Outright" to be read at his inauguration.[2] Kennedy's rise to power,
incidentally, overlapped with John Wayne's transformation from
movie star to cultural icon,[3] and in Slotkin's estimation, this
coincidence reveals, among other things, that "so long as the
nation-state remains the prevalent form of social organization,
something like a national myth/ideology will be essential to its
operations."[4] Thus, he concludes that Americans of all stripes,
wherever they happen to stand on the social-economic ladder or
fall on the political spectrum, instinctively make use of the myth

of the frontier and the ideology of redemptive violence, even on this side of the dramatic shifts of the civil rights era.

In 1968, Wayne directed and starred in *The Green Berets*, an anti-communist propaganda film intended to convince the American public of the validity and necessity of the war in Vietnam. Wayne's project, Slotkin argues, was "the logical fulfillment of the myth of charismatic leadership and counterinsurgency." But it failed, at least as a piece of propaganda, because the American consciousness had been altered by humiliations abroad and painful reckonings at home. The public no longer implicitly trusted "the Strong Man" to save "the weak people."[5] Still, even if "the light of American historical experience . . . exposed a fatal flaw in the original myth,"[6] the myth did not die. And the events of September 11, 2001, which Slotkin could not have foreseen, drove many back to their never fully abandoned belief in the need for "hunter-hero."

In a 2006 interview, David Milch, one of television's leading writers and showrunners, and the creator of *NYPD Blue* and *Deadwood*, discerned a familiar pattern developing in response to the trauma of the terrorist attacks:

> The assault on the collective sensibility of 9/11 was such as to give the audience so much fear that the only way that they could be placated was with a television series—a miniseries—which would be finished in three weeks and which would tell them that "You do not have to fear danger here because we are going to take the war over there." And the rationale for that war had nothing to do with weapons of mass destruction and everything to do with the habituation of the viewing public to the shaping of human experience in distorted forms for which the media is responsible. So that the first three weeks of the Iraq miniseries was received with *enormous* public approval because it was the series we wanted to see and it was the triumph of American weaponry and it had a beginning, a middle, and an end. And the disaffection with the Iraq war has nothing to do

with what is going on with the Iraqi people and everything
to do with the fact that that series is over. We don't want to
see that series anymore. We wanted to be narcotized in our
reaction to the assault on the World Trade Center. We got
what we were looking for.[7]

The televised events of the beginning of the "War on Terror,"
Milch suggests, was nothing but the staging of an escapist fiction,
a story intended to quell anxieties by numbing viewers to reality.
Because Americans have for so long been amusing themselves to
death, whenever and whatever they are made to fear, they find
themselves demanding a virtual experience that will expiate that
terror. After 9/11, that story had to be a retelling of The Story.

A Man without a Cross

Fifty years before Slotkin recognized and critiqued John Ford's John
Wayne, D. H. Lawrence recognized and critiqued James Fenimore
Cooper's Natty Bumppo as the central character in America's self-
defining myth. Bumppo—otherwise known as Deerslayer, Hawk-
eye, Pathfinder, Leatherstocking—is, in Lawrence's description, "an
isolate, almost selfless, stoic, enduring man, who lives by death, by
killing, but who is pure white." As a representative American, Cooper's hero is torn between innocence and lust, peace and violence,
civilization and the wilderness. On their behalf, in their stead, he is
made to live these contradictions to the utmost, which forces him
further and further outside the boundaries of acceptable norms. In
the last Leatherstocking story, Bumppo, at the end of his long life,
dies a noble, magnanimous death among the Pawnee. But in The
Prairie's last scene, he makes a final request and offers up a quietly
bitter complaint: "I am without kith or kin in the wide world . . .
When I am gone, there will be an end of my race . . . Let me sleep,
where I have lived, beyond the din of the settlements!" Bumppo,
anticipating John Wayne, is pure and a purist, the realization of an
ideal. But he suffers endlessly because of it. He remains as pristine
as the virgin and the wilderness, but is condemned to die alone
because of it. He is, as Slotkin says, "a man without a cross of sin

to bear, a man exempted from the fall, a new Adam. Yet he is also, implicitly, a man beyond the pale of Christianity, a man without the Cross to guide him." Caught between civilization and savagery, between the whites on the one hand and the natives on the other, the mythic hero cannot keep his purity without dying for it.[8]

It is easy to lose sight of the fact that our myths serve a vital purpose. Not only to justify what we have done and failed to do, but also to dress the wounds we have inflicted on ourselves by participation in oppression, exploitation, and violence. And that work is accomplished not only through the telling of exploits and victories of our heroes but also, and more decisively, through the telling of their death or exile. This is why the hero in George Stevens' *Shane* (1953) has to ride away in the end, ignoring the cries of the boy who idolizes him. "There's no living with a killing," he tells the boy. "There's no going back from one. Right or wrong, it's a brand. A brand sticks." And the same holds for Christopher Nolan's Batman in *The Dark Knight* (2008). The final scene mirrors almost exactly the end of *Shane*, revealing Batman as the heroic antihero, the exiled protector willing to do in the dark whatever is necessary for everyone else to live in the light. John Wayne's Ethan Edwards in John Ford's *The Searchers* (1956) suffers the same fate. After finally finding and rescuing Debbie, a white woman taken by savage Comanches, and restoring her to her family, Edwards finds he cannot return to civilized life. In the iconic closing scene, he stands at the door, forgotten, passed by, and then turns back to the wilderness as the door closes on his shadow. Edwards and Shane, like Bumppo and Boone, are condemned to die apart from the people they killed others to save. And this lays bare a crucial reality: the American myth, at least when courageously told and carefully read, is deeply ambiguous and fraught with irreconcilable differences. And in spite of Twain's snide remarks in his famous takedown of Cooper's "literary offenses," the characters in the Leatherstocking novels, like all mythic figures, must be "confusedly drawn," proving time and again by what they say and do that "they are not the sort of people the author claims they are," because they are necessarily constituted by contradictions.[9] And they are necessarily constituted by contradictions because their lives are a matrix in which our shared conflicts are proven, lived out toward their best or worst ends.

Kristin Kobes Du Mez argues that white evangelical support for Donald Trump's presidential candidacy and administration was neither unexpected nor merely pragmatic, but the culmination of evangelicals' long love affair with "militant masculinity." By Du Mez' account, white American evangelicals by and large hold to a "God-and-country faith" that affirms white supremacy, American exceptionalism, and Christian nationalism, moved by "a nostalgic yearning" for the reestablishment of a mythical social order embodied, paradigmatically, in John Wayne, the icon of "rugged American manhood."[10] But the story is quite a bit more complicated than Du Mez' critique allows. No doubt, John Wayne in some sense does iconize "militant masculinity" and "rugged individualism." And his image does at first glance invite adoration and imitation. But it always proves to be too much for anyone to live up to. The Strong Man's calling is absolutely forbidding. General MacArthur famously praised Wayne for his performance in *Sands of Iwo Jima* (1949), saying he represented the American serviceman "better than the American serviceman himself." But during the Vietnam War, veterans and physicians recognized that soldiers were buckling under the pressure to live up to that idealization of "superhuman military bravery, skill, and invulnerability to guilt and grief" and diagnosed them with "John Wayne Syndrome."[11] Du Mez is right to say "the cult of masculinity" defaces the gospel and rends the social fabric. And she is right to be concerned that so many outspoken evangelicals so blatantly disregard Jesus' teachings and pattern of life. Like Amy Fowler in *High Noon* (1952), a devout Quaker who abandons her religious convictions at the critical moment, shooting a bad man in the back in order to save her husband, American Christians do seem occasionally to shift allegiance more or less entirely from God to Caesar, at least for interruptions of time, whenever their way of life comes under threat. But it is an unfair and so misleading oversimplification to say, as does Du Mez, that American Evangelicals have simply substituted "a vengeful warrior Christ" for "the Jesus of the Gospels." And it is equally mistaken to say Americans adore John Wayne. Wayne, like his many predecessors and successors, is neither an icon nor an idol in any simple sense, at least not when his image is given its fullest expression. Like Boone and Bumppo, he is an archetype, a prevalent and prevailing image that emerged because it meets a need we feel to make sense of our lives in ways that make it easier for us to live with ourselves. And, as already said, the "hunter-hero," in spite of first appearances, turns out to be a man utterly at odds with himself, like Wayne's Edwards, haunted by the imperfect relation of nature and grace, fated to a life apart. As Springsteen sings in his "Song for Orphans," "lost souls search for saviors, but saviors don't last long." So, it is not that the lowly, peaceful Jesus has been recast in John Wayne's likeness as a vengeful warrior, but that Americans, at least those of us controlling and benefiting from its power structures, have not been able to free ourselves from our own conflictedness. We fear the nonviolent way of Jesus will not lead into the future we want for ourselves. And we fear his truthfulness will require us to reckon with our past. So, we need a John Wayne, a dark knight, to do the evil necessary to save us from evil, and then to pass into exile, bearing away our guilt.

Heroes and Saints

The ancient Feast of Epiphany, which hails the manifestation of Christ to the magi, his baptism by John, and his first miracle at the wedding in Cana, stands in the sharpest possible contrast with the American frontier myth and the doctrine of "manifest destiny." A Roman antiphon for the Magnificat at Vespers calls for worshippers to celebrate this day, which is "adorned by three miracles": "Today a star led the magi to the manger; today water was changed into wine at the wedding; today in the Jordan Christ willed to be baptized by John to save us, alleluia!"[12] And this trinity of miracles both testifies to Christ's identity and reveals his character, showing who he is, what he has been appointed to do, and how he purposes to accomplish it. At the beginning of his life, and again at the beginning of his ministry, he reveals himself not by what he says and does but by what he has said about and done to him. He submits to nature and its witness. He submits to the ministry of the prophet. He submits to the guidance of his mother. And what he receives turns out to be a gift to those who have given to him. As Maximus of Turin says in an Epiphany sermon: "Christ is baptized, not to be made holy by the water, but to make the water holy." And, as Peter Chrysologus says in one of his Epiphany sermons, Jesus forgives John not by touching him, but by submitting to his touch. The adoration of the magi matters for them and for us, not for Christ, signaling and securing their inclusion—and the inclusion of all "outsiders"—under his gracious rule.[13] And when Jesus turns water to wine for the guests at the wedding in Cana, he does so without drawing attention to himself—in the end, no one knows for sure what has happened except the servant who carried the jars—revealing his glory in the gladness he brings to others.

In all of these ways, the celebration of Epiphany reminds us that Christ is the hope of all who have been left to their suffering—the poor, the orphaned, the imprisoned, the impure, the outcast, the diseased—and the dread of those who have abused their powers and neglected those for whom they are responsible. Christ's story calls into question the coherence and validity of any myth of conquest and domination, including the Enlightenment myth of progress and the American myth of the frontier. So, at least for those who take his story as revelatory, the truth is unavoidable, however difficult it may be to confront: our good comes always only through the good we do for others, never from their humiliation or loss. The abundant life God desires for us comes not through predation but through sacrifice, not through the rout of our enemies or the claiming of their possessions but through care for them in their need and the sharing of our possessions with them. We are called to live not toward the future we imagine for ourselves but in the present that has actually come to us, not idealizing or whitewashing our past but seeking the reconciliation and restitution necessary for a full and fully shared flourishing.

America's mythic heroes are not exactly Christ figures, although they live in the shadow of the cross. It comes nearer the truth to say they are *dis*figured Christs who both reflect and distort Christian convictions about who we are, what we are bound to do, and how we are to live with one another in the world. We can see the effects of that distortion when we compare the stories of the hunter-hero with the stories of the saints. For a number of reasons, I find the stories of the Russian saints—Basil the Blessed, Seraphim of Sarov, Theophan the Recluse, Maria Skobtsova—particularly enlightening and poignant. And Eugene Vodolazkin's *Laurus* brings this tradition into focus with brilliant force. The novel tells a marvelously, hilariously unsettling story of tragedy, renunciation, pilgrimage, and repose, one which casts into sharp relief the difference between the myth of the frontier and traditional Christian understandings of the mature and venerable life.

In the book's first part, Arseny, an orphaned healer in late fifteenth-century Russia, loses his beloved grandfather, Christofer, and then, tragically, his secret lover and their son in childbirth. He flees in disgrace and terror. Seeking redemption, he takes his dead lover's name, Ustina, as his own and falls silent, living as a holy fool. After a long time, one of the other fools, Foma, urges him to change his pattern of life, and sends him on pilgrimage to a convent where Ustina, if she had lived, might have found her destiny: "Pray for her and for yourself. Be her and be yourself, simultaneously. Be outrageous." Then, he punches Arseny in the nose, and embraces him with a final word of warning: "By giving yourself to Ustina, you are, I know, exhausting your body; but disowning your body is only the half of it. As it happens, my friend, that can lead to pride." Stunned and bleeding, Arseny asks what more he can do. Foma whispers his reply in Arseny's ear: "Do more . . . Disown your identity. You have already taken the first step by calling yourself Ustin. So now disown yourself completely."[14]

Later, Arseny is sent out again on another, longer journey. Before he goes, Foma restores his identity with a final instruction: "Heale the ill by taking their sin upon yourself . . . And from now on you are not Ustin but Arseny, like before."[15] This pilgrimage takes him from Russia to Jerusalem and back again. And it also takes him through time. Along the way, he takes on new names, reinventing himself in the desire to redeem others. He works miracles, although not for everyone. He cares for the needy when he can, although sometimes he can only cry and kiss them tenderly. But he never feels sure of himself or certain of his redemption. As he says to his friend,

> For many years, I have been attempting to devote myself to saving Ustina, whom I killed. And I still just cannot understand if my effort is beneficial. I keep waiting for some sort of sign that could show me I am going in the right direction, but I have not seen a single sign in all these years . . . I am just afraid, Ambrogio, that everything I am doing is not helping Ustina and my path is leading me away from her, not toward her.

Only after he has returned home from Jerusalem does he learn the truth: Christ is the only direction, the only destination, that matters. Near the end of his life, after he has been given his last name, Laurus shares the hard-won wisdom with Anastasia—a poor, unmarried, pregnant girl who has come to him for salvation. Comforting her, he shares the story of Alexander the Great, a story he loves to tell, explaining that the hero's conquests and explorations were all for nothing. Then he whispers in her ear, just as the holy fool Foma had whispered to him so long ago: "Life has no historical goal."[16]

The Only Turning

Paul Thomas Anderson's *There Will Be Blood* (2007), loosely based on Upton Sinclair's novel *Oil!*, delivers a searing condemnation of American mythology. The archetypal and almost too aptly named Daniel Plainview and Eli Sunday—one a prospector, the other a preacher—in turn discover that neither the blood of the Lamb nor the blood of the land can save them. And in the film's final scene, Plainview murders Sunday much as Cain murdered Abel, bludgeoning him to death, then collapsing on the floor beside him. When the butler comes down the stairs to see what has happened, Plainview acknowledges, calmly: "I'm finished"—a mockery of Christ's last words and an admission of his hopelessness. If, as Slotkin claims, myths are a means by which we make sense of our shared history, working out our contradicting beliefs and incompatible convictions, then Anderson's film counsels despair: what we have made of our history shows that we do not believe it is possible to share a history.

Will Arbery's award-winning play *Heroes of the Fourth Turning* offers a slightly more hopeful account of the American experiment. Arbery's characters, like many of their contemporary Americans, live haunted, tormented lives. At least a few of them feel their way of life is under threat. And as a result, they believe they must defend it or risk losing everything that matters to them. Near the end of the play, Teresa, having had too much to drink, faces off against Dr. Presson, one of her intellectual heroes. She believes her former teacher has lost her nerve: "We're in Crisis. They're coming for our tabernacle. They want to burn it down. They want to destroy the legacy of heroes like you. So I propose leveling up . . . Going blow for blow. And being ready for the war, if it happens. *When* it happens."[17] Dr. Presson's response is withering, but her idealism, livid with condescension, betrays her. Only her disabled daughter, Emily, seems truly open to reality. She is far from perfect, of course. Like her mother and her friends, she is naive and pretentious, even puerile at times. But she bears a gift: she feels others' pain intently. She can do nothing about what she feels. And she is not sure if she wants to feel it. But precisely because she shows a willingness to hold those experiences helplessly, she shines with Christ's light, just as Arseny does. She radiates, at least in these moments, something of what Rahner describes as the essence of Christian maturity: "openness of spirit, freedom from fanaticism, a willingness to learn, a mastery of one's own aggressiveness, and patience."[18] And that openness, that freed and freeing self-control, is the mark not of heroism but saintliness. As Samuel Wells explains, heroes are the center and circumference of their stories, and their stories are always stories of triumph and glory. The hero may fail, but he "knows no repentance." Saints, by contrast, live in a story not their own, less admirably but more honestly. Just so, their many failures are graced, opening out on "the cycle of repentance, forgiveness, reconciliation, and restoration" that Christians recognize as the pattern of life God's death makes possible.[19] This is at the heart of the faith Christians have received: in what Christ suffered God has made it possible for even heroes—those whose lives are lived in total opposition to the Spirit and the kingdom of God—to become saints.

At the end of the Coen brothers' *No Country for Old Men* (2007), Tommy Lee Jones' Sheriff Ed Tom Bell confesses that he feels overmatched and undone by the sheer senselessness of the violence he has witnessed. But his confessor reproves him: "What you got ain't nothin' new. This country is hard on people. You can't stop what's comin'. Ain't all waitin' on you. That's vanity." It is precisely vanity that Arseny is saved from in the end. Unlike the heroes who make a name for themselves, Arseny takes the names of others, those he desires to help in whatever way he can. "In that giving room, Arseny becomes not only more fully himself, but a place where very many others can find life too."[20] He acquires the Spirit of peace, and the souls of so many find their salvation in him. He does this by assuming not their identity but sharing their moral vocation, acting in their stead and on their behalf. Like Jacob, he wrestles—but not with God so much as with himself.

And like Jacob, he is a man of more than one name, names which together reveal his destiny. He is like Jacob, but he is not a Christ figure. He is, instead, a man touched by the figure of Christ as Jacob was, a man always striving to figure what his life means in the light of the darkness of Good Friday. Just so, he offers a true alternative to Daniel Boone, Natty Bumppo, John Wayne, and our other heroes. He does share much in common with them: He lives a life apart; he bears unusual gifts and suffers unusual losses and pains; he is deeply conflicted, living at odds with himself. He is a pilgrim and an explorer—but not a hunter and even less a conqueror. Most of all, he knows he is no hero. He cannot save anyone, even if he can and must suffer with them and for them. He is, in a word, humbled, stripped of vanity. He is a man with a cross. So, in the end, Arseny does not look out into the dark but into the fire—and has an epiphany, seeing himself: he is a child, like the child he lost, like the child who came to save him. And when he dies, he does not die alone.

4

God's Scars

Ash Wednesday

The binding of Isaac was man's test of God.
Elie Wiesel

Go and learn what this means, "I desire mercy, not sacrifice."
Matthew 9:13

Racism will disappear when it's no longer profitable and no longer psychologically useful.
Toni Morrison

Odysseus' Scar and Abraham's Sacrifice

"Everything remains unexpressed." In this line from his *Mimesis*, a book that more or less established the discipline of comparative literature, Erich Auerbach, a self-identified "Prussian of the Mosaic faith," names the crucial distinction between the Homeric and biblical narratives.[1] He finds this difference in the contrast between a passage in book 19 of *The Odyssey* and the story of the Akedah—Abraham's sacrifice of Isaac in Genesis 22.

In the revealing Homeric scene, "Odysseus has at last come home," and his old housekeeper and former nurse, Euryclea, recognizes a scar on his thigh as she washes his feet.

No sooner has the old woman touched the scar than, in her joyous surprise, she lets Odysseus' foot drop into the basin;

the water spills over, she is about to cry out her joy; Odysseus restrains her with whispered threats and endearments; she recovers herself and conceals her emotion. Penelope, whose attention Athena's foresight had diverted from the incident, has observed nothing.[2]

Auerbach observes how this scene is "scrupulously externalized and narrated in leisurely fashion." Everything is expressed, he says. "Clearly outlined, brightly and uniformly illuminated, men and things stand out in a realm where everything is visible; and not less clear—wholly expressed, orderly even in their ardor . . ." He observes, too, that there is nothing, or almost nothing, in this style intended to generate or sustain suspense for the reader. On the contrary, the tension is purposefully eased. Action is not arrested or pushed back; it is simply replaced with another act in turn, which is also meant to hold the reader's attention completely. In book 19, for example, just after the housekeeper recognizes the stranger's scar, the narrator digresses to the account of the hunt in which Odysseus was wounded as a boy. But not only the hunt, also the arrival at his grandfather's house is described in detail, as are the house itself, his grandfather's character, Odysseus' arrival at the estate, the greetings exchanged, the banquet at which he was introduced, the early morning start of the hunt, the tracking of the boar, the struggle that leaves the young Odysseus injured, the response to his wounds by those who love him, his recovery and return home, etc. Only then does the story return to Euryclea and Odysseus in Penelope's room.

Auerbach sums up Homeric style as "uniformly illuminated." It gives the reader "a complete externalization of all the elements of the story and of their interconnections as to leave nothing in obscurity." It "knows only a foreground." Biblical style, by contrast, he argues, is "fraught with background." The story of Abraham's near sacrifice, for example, is mysterious not only at its beginning and end, not only in what God says and does, but at every point along the way. In Auerbach's words, the story itself "unrolls with no episodes in a few independent sentences whose syntactical connection is of the most rudimentary sort."[3] A terrible deed is required. The place where it must be done is decided. Abraham offers no protest. He awakes early, gathers what is needed, and then he and his son and two servants make the journey. Sarah is never mentioned. The journey takes three days. Only after they arrive does anyone speak: Isaac only asks questions and Abraham speaks only in half-truths. On the mountaintop, the father builds the altar and binds his son to it, without a word passing between them. At last, he raises the knife—and the angel of the Lord intervenes, directing his attention to a ram caught by its horns in a thicket. Abraham takes it, sacrificing it instead of his son, and afterward names the place, The Lord Will Provide, and the angel blesses him in God's name. Finally, he returns, apparently alone, to the servants who have been waiting, and the three of them make their way home without a word. Isaac seems to have been forgotten—by his father and the servants, at least, if not also the reader. At last mention, he was still bound to the altar.

The contrast with *The Odyssey* could hardly be sharper. As Auerbach observes, Homeric characters speak in order to express their thoughts. And what they say casts light on the world they inhabit, a world already entirely unhidden, fully manifested, perfectly detailed. Biblical characters, however, speak only "to indicate thoughts which remain unexpressed."[4] God's purposes are never revealed, at least not clearly. At first, the reader knows only that God "tested" Abraham, which is surprising given that God has already made it clear that he knows Abraham's future and trusts Abraham's character implicitly. At last, Abraham is told his obedience has indeed won him a blessing—the same blessing already given and reaffirmed no less than five times. Throughout the ordeal, and even after it, Abraham's thoughts and feelings remain unknown. And the same goes for Isaac, about whom we know next to nothing except that Abraham loves him—obviously in a way God does not.

It would be difficult, then, to imagine styles more contrasted than those of these two equally ancient and equally epic texts. On the one hand, externalized, uniformly illuminated phenomena, at a definite time and in a definite place, connected together without lacunae in a perpetual foreground; thoughts and feeling completely expressed; events taking place in leisurely fashion and with very little of suspense. On the other hand, the externalization of only so much of the phenomena as is necessary for the purpose of the narrative, all else left in obscurity; the decisive points of the narrative alone are emphasized, what lies between is nonexistent; time and place are undefined and call for interpretation; thoughts and feelings remain unexpressed, are only suggested by the silence and the fragmentary speeches; the whole, permeated with the most unrelieved suspense and directed toward a single goal (and to that extent far more of a unity), remains mysterious and "fraught with background."[5]

Auerbach notices that Homeric style shows "the complexity of the psychological life" only in the succession of emotions. Characters are either afraid or relieved, either unhappy or overjoyed. But the stories in the Jewish Scriptures "express the simultaneous existence of various layers of consciousness and the conflict between them." In short, everything is infinitely "backgrounded." Whatever is said or done is "entangled and stratified." And God is behind and before and after and in the midst of it all, manifest and hidden, speaking and holding silent, coming and going, revealing and concealing, restoring and destroying. This, Auerbach explains, is why biblical figures develop over time, while Homeric figures, like Odysseus and Achilles and Agamemnon, do not: "The stern hand of God is ever upon the Old Testament figures; he has not only made them once and for all and chosen them, but he continues to work upon them, bends them and kneads them, and, without destroying them in essence, produces

from them forms which their youth gave no grounds for anticipating."[6] Because God is in the midst of it all, sometimes strongly,
sometimes weakly, the sublime and the mundane become inti-
mately, indistinguishably, co-determined.

The upshot of the differences between Homer and Scripture,
Auerbach concludes, is that the former can be analyzed but not
interpreted, while the latter forbids analysis and requires interpretation. Scripture, at least as Auerbach reads it, exerts a kind
of violence on the reader: "The Bible's claim to truth is not only
far more urgent than Homer's, it is tyrannical."[7] The biblical stories, like the volatile but purposeful God they witness, show no
interest in entertainment. They want only to quell our rebellion,
to "overcome our reality." Or so Auerbach contends. But there
are other, perhaps more generous and generative construals of
what Scripture is doing. He is right, I believe, about how the
story of the binding of Isaac differs from the story of Euryclea
discovering Odysseus' scar. But he is ever so slightly wrong, I
believe, about *why* everything remains unexpressed. He says
the Akedah, like other stories in Scripture, is violent. And he is
right about that. But it is not tyrannical. In fact, it is restrained:
we are not. We cannot make sense of everything we are seeing; at times, we can hardly make sense of any of it. But it is
being shown to us, nonetheless, and that fact compels us to try
to understand. All to say, what Auerbach misses is that the story
does not do to us what God did to his friend or what Abraham
did to his servants, his wife, and his son. It does not leave us in
the dark: it shows us the darkness.

This is a critical point. In Plato's allegory, the prisoners, once
freed, seek to leave the cave but are dazzled by the light and
driven back to the darkness by the fire of the sun. In Moses'
story, however we are not blinded; the narrative makes possible
an awareness of the background in which we are forced to live.
We are made to see that there is much we cannot see, made to
hear the silence that hides a conversation carried on without us.

And not only that: this story, told as it is, frees us up to test these characters, to question their motives, to doubt their purposes, to require them to say what has been left unsaid, so that we can do what needs next to be done. The knife is in our hand, so to speak, and God, as it were, is on the altar.

Christian readers, even the most skilled and learned ones, struggle to read this story the way I believe it wants to be read. Aquinas, for instance, raises the question about the rightness of Abraham's obedience only to insist that it should not be asked, not because hard questions should be avoided but because it is analytically nonsensical. God's command makes right, right and wrong, wrong. So, whatever God says should be done is by definition rightly done. It may seem, Aquinas admits, that slaying the innocent is always wrong, as adultery and theft are always wrong. But God requires exactly that of Abraham, just as he required Hosea to "take a wife of whoredom" (Hos 1:2) and Israel to plunder the Egyptians (Exod 12:35). He insists, therefore, that Abraham was right to obey God without question, because by God's command "death can be inflicted on any man, guilty or innocent, without any injustice."[8]

Kierkegaard's more famous, more daring, reading is no less problematic. For Aquinas, the sacrifice itself was good because God had commanded it. Or, more to the point, Abraham was right to be willing to sacrifice his son because God had commanded it. For Kierkegaard, it was Abraham's *willingness* to sacrifice his son that can be called good. Indeed, it was sublime—and precisely because he did what was asked of him without deliberation, even though it was unthinkable, unconscionable, abhorrent.[9] Aquinas wants to insist that what Abraham was willing to do was not wrong. Kierkegaard wants to insist that Abraham's willingness is impressive precisely because what he willed so daringly would otherwise have been wrong. Abraham is justified by his faith, but only because he refuses every grace.

The Augustinian scholar, James Wetzel, rightly rejects both of these readings. And he suggests a shocking alternative:

Does Abraham remember Sarah when raising his cleaver? I can't help but think that he does, that he is more knowing than a knight of faith, that he is shrewder than an unquestioning servant to a divine patriarch. He is an awakened Adam. It seems to me that the choice at the heart of the Akedah is finally not Abraham's but Yahweh's. This God can claim his share in the life of his son by making the woman's share his own, or he can let the woman be his otherness and have his son with her. When Abraham raises a cleaver and forces the issue, it is not Abraham's faith that keeps him from becoming a murderer but his prescience.[10]

God, in other words, is the one who is tested. Now, Abraham knows God will let nothing, not even his own commands, keep him from fulfilling his promises.

Moriah, Sinai, Golgotha

Although Wetzel seems not to know it, this is almost exactly the reading of the story that Elie Wiesel offers. For him, this story, even more than the story of Sinai, defines what it means to be a Jew. It contains, he says, "Jewish destiny in its totality." In a famous chapter, Wiesel recounts how as a child he read and reread this story, overtaken by "dark apprehension." Questions flooded out of him: "Why would God, the merciful Father, demand that Abraham become inhuman, and why would Abraham accept?" Why does Isaac mutely go along with it? What can it mean to call Abraham "father" if he is willing to do this to his son—and even without protest? And how sickening that the most tragic figure in Scripture is named Laughter.[11]

Wiesel's own horrifying experiences during the Shoah only intensified these apprehensions. He survived, as Isaac did. His father did not. As André Neher observes, Wiesel's *Night* is "an Akeda in reverse: not a father leading his son to the sacrifice, but a son conducting, dragging, carrying to the sacrifice an old, exhausted father."[12] In his cantata, *Ani Ma'amin*, Wiesel gives Abraham these lines to sing to God—or, more accurately, at him:

The Torah forbids
The slaughter of an animal
And its young
On the same day.
Yet—fathers and sons
Are massacred
In each other's presence
Every day. Is then a Jew
Less precious
Than a beast?[13]

All along, Wiesel says, he identified with Isaac, "the first survivor." But only late in life did he come to love Isaac's father, who is, of course, his own forefather. Grappling with their story and with his own, poring over the traditional readings, listening to the witness of his own heart and the testimonies of other survivors, Wiesel eventually realized that Abraham, who had long before stood up to God for the sake of Lot, his nephew, and Ishmael, his firstborn, must have been testing God as surely God was testing him: "God subjected Abraham to it, yet at the same time Abraham forced it on God. As though Abraham had said: I defy You, Lord. I shall submit to Your will, but let us see whether You shall go to the end, whether You shall remain passive and remain silent when the life of my son—who is also Your son—is at stake!" In the end, at the decisive moment, God relented. "Abraham won." And that, Wiesel quips, is why God sent the angel to stay Abraham's hand: he was too embarrassed to show his own face.[14]

Abraham bested God at his own game, not once but three times. According to a midrashic reading, which Wiesel holds up, Abraham demands the intervening angel prove he is God's and not Satan's. When he cannot, Abraham insists God speak for himself: if he gave the order to slay an innocent, then he must rescind it in person, not through an emissary. As this midrash has it, once God personally acknowledges that he rescinds the order, embarrassing himself a second time, Abraham tests him yet again, insisting that just as he obeyed God's will in this matter without saying a word; so, in the future, when his innumerable children, whom God had promised to give him, fail to obey, God must forgive them without a word: "So be it, God agreed, Let them but retell this tale and they will be forgiven."[15]

So understood, Abraham's faith is for Wiesel a witness to the way God calls Israel to live. But Isaac's faith is greater still, because, after he survived, in spite of everything, he did not "rebel against life." He is known as "the defender of his people" not because he suffered—suffering, Wiesel notes, "confers no privileges," at least not on Jews—but because he, without rancor or bitterness, transformed his suffering into gift, into sacrifice, into love, into prayer. Haunted, he nonetheless "remained capable of laughter." And this is what won him favor with God. "His reward? The Temple was built on Moriah. Not on Sinai."[16] For Wiesel, this is the heart of Jewishness, the heart of the graceful life: to live for life, to live for the living. We cannot say "Here I am" to our God if we do not say it also to our neighbor.

Christians, as I have said, tend to take this text at face value—and applaud themselves for facing it. Wiesel suspects that this is because they read in Isaac's binding "a prefiguration of the crucifixion." But he insists that what happens on Moriah is nothing at all like what happened on Golgotha: "on Mount Moriah the act was *not* consummated: the father did *not* abandon his son." And the difference is definitive: "no man has the right to sacrifice another, not even to God."

> Had he killed his son, Abraham would have become the forefather of a people—but not the Jewish people. For the Jew, all truth must spring from life, never from death. To us, crucifixion represents not a step forward but a step backward: at the top of Moriah, the living remains alive, thus marking the end of an era of ritual murder. To invoke the *Akeda* is tantamount to calling for mercy—whereas from the beginning Golgotha has served as a pretext for countless massacres for sons and fathers cut down together by

sword and fire in the name of a word that considered itself synonymous with love.[17]

As Wiesel reads it, the story of Isaac's binding is also the story of his—and our—loosing. The son and the father are scarred, each in his own way. But so is God. The story of Jesus, however, is a story not of the living, wounded and freed; it is a story of the glorification of death. Isaac's story, Wiesel insists, negates forever the possibility of human sacrifice. But Jesus' story, as the Christians tell it, attempts to negate that negation. Christians affirm, knowingly or not, the reinstatement of ritual murder.

Wiesel's critique should not be brushed aside. But, again, other readings of what happens on Golgotha are possible. Paul seems to refer to the Akedah near the end of Romans 8, boasting in God's protection and provision: "If God is for us, who is against us? He who did not withhold his own Son, but gave him up for all of us, will he not with him also give us everything else?" (Rom 8:31-32). Closely read, this is seen not to be a story of death, at least not in the sense Wiesel fears. Indeed, it is not the reversal of Isaac's story, but its divine reprise. In it, God does not require a sacrifice of us: he makes one for us. And he makes it only so that through it he might give us his own life. Jesus dies, to be sure. But not because the Father takes his life or abandons him to death. That is precisely the point: his life cannot be taken, because his life is nothing other than the bond he has with the Father, a bond that is inviolable, because it is nothing other than the Spirit, who *is* life (Rom 8:10). Thus, nothing can separate us from God any more than it can separate God from God. And no matter that we so often hear the story told otherwise: Golgotha is neither an act of God against us nor an act of God against God for us. It is the act of God with God with us against death and all deathly powers. It is a sacrifice, yes; but what makes it what it is, is that it is a sacrifice in which "the living remains alive"—*in death*, and "after" it.

In the final analysis, then, Wiesel is not exactly wrong: Christians do tend to read this story falsely. Perhaps our familiarity with and affection for at least some version of the story of Jesus' death makes it so that the story of Isaac's near death fails to affect us as it should. Or perhaps our casual disregard for anything "Old Testament" as primitive makes it seem like something we have simply outgrown. Or perhaps the terse strangeness of the story simply defeats us. In any case, Christian readings often settle either for what is wrongly thought to be the plain sense, or for some spiritualized reading that glances off the face of the story. But Paul's reading, and the reading of Hebrews, perhaps the two earliest Christian interpretations, succeed where our readings mostly fail.

Augustine argues that the handing over of the Son in Romans 8:32 is prefigured in the story of Isaac. He is convinced Abraham did not and could not have believed God delights in human sacrifices. And he is also convinced Abraham never once wavered in his belief that God's promise would be fulfilled through Isaac. So, Augustine concludes, Abraham obeys the command to offer up his son only because he believed God would raise him up again after he died. He finds confirmation of this in Hebrews 11:17-19: "By faith Abraham, when put to the test, offered up Isaac. He who had received the promises was ready to offer up his only son, of whom he had been told, 'It is through Isaac that descendants shall be named for you.' He considered the fact that God is able even to raise someone from the dead—and figuratively speaking, he did receive him back."[18]

But Hebrews does not quite say what Augustine takes it to mean. It does not say merely that Abraham, who was himself "as good as dead" (Heb 11:12), was willing to offer up his son, but that he actually did so—and received him back again. His sacrifice, then, was true; because, like Abel's and unlike Cain's, it was offered in spirit. In other words, Abraham readily obeyed because he knew all along that God had commanded not the ritual murder of his son but a liturgical prefiguration of Jesus' future self-offering. In this sense, Abraham is like Moses: he relates to Jesus ahead of time. And by virtue of that relationship, what Abraham did, he did not only on Moriah but also on the invisible Zion (Heb

12:22), "looking ahead," beyond the things seen to the things not seen (Heb 11:1). He foresaw, by faith, the promises; therefore, he knew how to pre-enact their fulfillment. It is in this sense that Abraham is the father of faith.

Fanciful as this reading may seem at first, it fits with Hebrews' claims about the self-offering of Jesus. In a shocking passage, we are told Jesus came into the world praying a Psalm of deep conflictedness: "Sacrifices and offerings you have not desired, but a body you have prepared for me" (Heb 10:5). He knows God has no need of sacrifice. And yet—that is exactly what he makes of himself. Why? Hebrews insists, again and again, that religious systems—including, even, especially, *the* Law—cannot "set things right" (Heb 9:10). The perfect Law, perfectly enacted, does not perfect the law keepers, much less the lawbreakers. Thus, there is a need for something "better" to be done, something lasting and effectual, which will alter our consciousness at its roots, setting our hearts at last at ease, freeing us up to live and die unanxiously, as Jesus did, before God and with God. And that, Hebrews concludes, is precisely what Jesus accomplishes, offering himself to God as he did, not in order to satisfy the demands of the Law but in order to alter us, our sense of ourselves, and our sense of how the world works, not merely shifting our perspective but also curing our core perceptivity. In the language of Hebrews, our consciences are sprinkled clean in his blood. God's Law has been written into our hearts—seeded in our subconscious—so that his will begins over time to come more and more naturally to us.

Right from the first, Hebrews declares that we do not hold this awareness; it holds us. Jesus, the one who is unchanging, sustains all things, bearing them along toward God's purposes for them (Heb 1:3). So, Hebrews argues, he will bear us "outside the city" (Heb 13:12) to live as he did and does—as strangers, aliens, pioneers, priests of a different order. Over time, as we are making ourselves at home in that "outside," learning to distance ourselves from the life we were told we should want to live, we begin to sense a growing awareness that there is for us, as well as for everyone and everything else, a future constituted by nothing less than the full outworking of God's inner life—"a lasting city," "a city not made with hands," "a city that is to come," "the city of the living God." That, according to Hebrews, is what it means to live by faith.

Hebrews is abundantly clear that what we do, or fail to do, matters. God says to Abraham, "Because you have done this . . . I will indeed bless you." But this is only after God has offered a preface: "By myself I have sworn . . ." (Gen 22:16). And this is not lost on the writer of Hebrews: "When God made a promise to Abraham, because he had no one greater by whom to swear, he swore by himself . . ." (Heb 6:13). And the writer concludes that *that* is what effected Abraham's faithfulness: "And thus, Abraham, having patiently endured, obtained the promise" (Heb 6:15). Later, we read that Abraham died without receiving the promise (Heb 11:13, 39). Yet, in some sense, Hebrews holds he had already obtained it. How? Perhaps because in facing down death, receiving his son by the same act in which he gave him up, Abraham recognized Jesus and knew him as the one who had already accomplished everything we have yet to experience.

The Death of Sacrifice

For the writer of Hebrews, it is precisely through his death—his bloody death—that Jesus saves us. Not, as we might think, by meeting some lawful demand for bloodshed, much less by satisfying some divine bloodthirstiness. No, Jesus saves us by destroying the fear of death, which evil has always used against us to our hurt and the hurt of others. "Since, therefore, the children share flesh and blood, he himself likewise shared the same things, so that through death he might destroy the one who has the power of death, that is, the devil, and free those who all their lives were held in slavery by the fear of death" (Heb 2:14-15). Because we are so weakly familiar with this story, we have to make ourselves attend to the fact that Jesus did not simply die. His death did not magically do wonders. He lived into death, prayerfully, soulfully. As Hebrews

says, "In the days of his flesh, Jesus offered up prayers and suppli-
cations, with loud cries and tears, to the one who was able to save
him from death, and he was heard because of his reverent submission" (Heb 5:7). To say that he was heard by the one who was able
to save him from death is to say he trusted himself so completely
to God that he died without dying. Or, put differently, it is to say
that he was saved not from dying but from death. In fact, according to Hebrews, this is exactly what makes his intercession different from anyone else's: "the former priests were many in number,
because they were prevented by death from continuing in office;
but he holds his priesthood permanently, because he continues forever" (Heb 7:23-24). He died, and was dead. And yet, "he always
lives" (Heb 7:25). This does not mean that his "human side" ceased
to exist while his "divine side" went on existing. It means that he
died, exactly as we do, but in that moment entrusted himself to
God in a way we cannot, so that his death, his creaturely nonexis-
tence, became an integral part of his work on our behalf, ensuring
for us that death is nothing to fear, because it is nothing but a way
opened, like a wound, into the Son's uncreated intimacy with God
by his own wounded flesh (Heb 10:19-20).

Precisely because it anticipates the future only God can make,
faith can afford to be happy in the present tense. It can be honest
about the past, and about the "multilayeredness" of our lives—the
entanglements and stratifications that complicate our relationships and thwart so much of what we most deeply want to do for
one another. Faith, as Hebrews conceives it, can be honest about
failures and about weaknesses. It can be honest about family. And
it can be honest about all of this because first it is honest about
death. So, Ash Wednesday, which is the time set aside each year
for us to face our mortality directly—a fact sealed by our letting
someone leave a mark of that mortality on our faces for others to
see—is a perfect day to have the Akedah read to us. The oily, ashy
crosses on our foreheads are a reminder of the ways that Jesus is
the son of Abraham and Sarah and therefore Isaac's brother, and

that his sacrifice confirms that Abraham was right to say God does not want ritual murder.

We have to be so careful right at this point. Hebrews is notoriously difficult to interpret, and without question there are anti-Jewish and Marcionite ways of handling this text. In fact, many, perhaps most, Christians have taken Hebrews to mean that the "Old Testament" and all that it represents is best left behind. But read carefully, Hebrews leads us not away from the faith of Abraham and his descendants but deeper into it. And it does this by teaching us to give all of our attention to the texts of Israel's Scriptures. From the first, the writer situates Jesus in the very center of the being and act of God, identifying him as the Son through whom and for whom all things were made and the "exact imprint of God's very being" (Heb 1:2-3). But even before doing this, he makes it clear that that center exists at the heart of the story of Israel. The God in whom Christ lives is Israel's God, the God who spoke to the fathers through the prophets (Heb 1:1). Christ identifies himself with us precisely in "the midst of the congregation" (Heb 2:12). And he comes to help, not angels, but "the descendants of Abraham" (Heb 2:16).

At the last, the writer urges us to "look to" Jesus, to consider him (Heb 12:2-3). But he has already made it clear that we will not recognize Jesus if we do not see him first in the stories Israel's Scriptures tell. This is why Hebrews 11 begins with the story of the creation and then moves through the stories of Abel, Enoch, and Noah into the stories of the call of Abraham and his life with Sarah, the stories of Isaac and Jacob and Esau, and, finally, Joseph, before turning to the life of Moses, which opens out on crucial events in Israel's history: the Passover, the Exodus, and the Conquest. He concludes with an allusive torrent of references to the lives of Israel's judges, kings, and prophets. Then, he reveals that this "great cloud of witnesses" speaks with one voice, directing our attention to Jesus (Heb 12:1) who manifests himself not on Sinai, which, for all its glory, was merely a station in the wilderness, but in Zion—the political heart of the finally fully established kingdom of God. Jesus' blood "speaks a better word" than Abel's and effects a "better covenant" (Heb 12:24) only in the sense that through his death, he accomplishes the realization of every hope—not only Israel's hopes for God, but also God's hopes for Israel, as the people through whom the whole creation is blessed. All to say, if we hope to think and feel and talk and act Christianly about death, we shall have to do it Jewishly.

In this, Simone Weil could not be more misguided. She contends the Gospels are "the last marvelous expression of the Greek genius, as the *Iliad* is the first." And as she reads them, the Evangelists, like Homer, are poets of force, showing how "a divine spirit, incarnate, is changed by misfortune, trembles before suffering and death, feels itself, in the depths of its agony, to be cut off from man and God." But her anti-Semitism distorts her vision, not only of the texts but also of her own and others' lived experience. She finds in Homer a world fully realized, one without background, and so a world absolutely constrained, a world in which fate and providence are two names for one reality. Thus, she concludes the misery one feels because of these constraints is "a pre-condition of justice and love," because only through attention to this misery is one freed from self-deception.

Weil laments that none of this is found in the Old Testament (except, she says, for parts of the book of Job). But that is because, as we have seen, the world Israel inhabits is one of unbelievable freedom and equally unbelievable vulnerability. In this world, compassion, not misery, is the precondition of justice. The prophets lament that Israel lacks *hesed*—"steadfast love." What matters, they contend, is not self-knowing but the acknowledgment of God in the enactment of justice. Weil is right to call into question the Christian myth of pious self-sacrifice and the practices of forceful proselytization. She is right to say that if God himself "could not face the harshness of destiny without a long tremor of anguish," then it is blasphemous to imagine we or anyone else can or should ascend to a "higher plane," rising above ordinary human misery.[19] She is wrong, however, to think that "the Greeks" knew this and that "the Hebrews" and "the Romans" did not. And she is wrong to think that human misery is what reveals the truth of our condition. It is knowing the misery of God that moves us to do justice.

Sacrificing Art

That returns us, finally, to the contrast between Homeric and biblical narrative. If, as I have argued, the aim of the scriptural texts is to bring the "background" to our awareness, to compel us to see the darkness, and to probe it; and if, as the New Testament claims, Jesus is the fulfillment of Israel's desires, then his story does not drive away that darkness in which we move, but deepens it, assuring us that it is not the void, not the manifestation of the devourer, but simply the thick, deep, terrifying darkness that is the unapproachable light in which God does what God alone can do. Still, even after we have seen and heard that the infinite background in which our lives happen is nothing other than the heart of God for us, his devotion to us, we have to admit that it is background and it is infinite. That fact should give shape not only to our reading of Scripture and our praying, but also to the making and appreciation of our art.

R. S. Thomas' "Souillac: Le Sacrifice d' Abraham" calls attention to an engraving in the central pillar of the huge double doors, which once led into a medieval abbey church. The engraving is in fact a detail within a larger sculpture: Abraham and his son are entangled in twisting, writhing figures of monsters and beasts, all cut from a single block of stone. Thomas suggests this entanglement not only in the opening line, but even from the first word:

> And he grasps him by the hair
> With innocent savagery.
> And the son's face is calm;
> There is trust there.
>
> And the beast looks on.
>
> This is what art could do,
> Interpreting faith
> With serene chisel.
> The resistant stone
> Is quiet as our breath,
> And is accepted.[20]

Visually, the poem is column-like. But more importantly, it mimics or reenacts something of the engraving's innate stillness and austerity. In the opening line, for example, the poem grasps us, just as the man grasps the boy's hair—suggesting a violence that never in fact arrives. And in the last line, we take Isaac's acceptance as our own just as he had taken his father's acceptance as his own.

Remarkably, both the poem and the engraving are stylistically matched to the biblical narrative, a fact which sets them in sharp contrast with other representations of the scene, including, for example, Caravaggio's and Rembrandt's astonishing paintings. But neither the paintings, nor the poem, nor the engraving merely repeats the Genesis story without a difference. They *represent* it, and in that way suggest ways of seeing and hearing that story differently. In both Caravaggio's and Rembrandt's paintings, Abraham is fiercely intent on the task, oblivious to the ram presented to save him from what he is doing. Isaac, we see, has already suffered everything he can suffer. Death would only be a release from this trauma. But in the sculpture, Abraham's head is cocked severely, in an attitude of extreme curiosity. He seems entranced. The knife is raised, but not at all threateningly, and his other hand clasps his young son's hair, but again without violence. Isaac leans into his father; eyes closed, but not tightly; head resting gently against his father's lowered chest; hands pressed gently together and held out in front of himself, caringly, as if in prayer. In these ways, this work shows us how this moment might be imagined otherwise—not as an unthinkable terror, but as something unfathomably tender.

That, one might argue, is what Thomas' poem suggests art can and should do, if it is marked by grace. It can show us how resistance becomes acceptance without violence. But that is not to say that art—including liturgical art—should not represent the violence. It means only that that violence should be represented in ways that "otherwise" it. For example, the mosaic in the Byzantine Basilica of San Vitale, like the Souillac engraving and unlike the Caravaggio and Rembrandt paintings, shows Abraham standing not over but beside Isaac, his left hand resting lightly on the child's head, his sword hand raised, but without intent. He looks demandingly into the heavens as if to ask if this is truly what God desires. But the mosaic in the twelfth-century Palatine Chapel shows Abraham towering over Isaac, wrenching back his son's head into an impossible position, his knife already thrusting at his son's throat, utterly caught off guard by the angelic intervention. At the left side of the mosaic, however, *Jesus* is the one shown to have commanded Abraham to take his beloved child and slay him. This makes all the difference, both returning us to the stories of Scripture with an eye for Jesus and returning us to the story of Jesus with the eye of Scripture. And it is that difference which makes the difference between true and false, worthy and unworthy, liturgy and liturgical art.

Of course, many of our churches lack liturgical art. And perhaps that is not unrelated to the fact that sometimes what we do lacks artfulness. Be that as it may, Ash Wednesday should be a time not merely to reflect on our mortality in and of itself, but to think about how we are implicated in God's mortality, a thought which we can think Christianly only as it is shepherded by the story of Jesus, which is impossible to tell rightly apart from the story of Israel. If, then, as Thomas' poem suggests, art can imitate the life of these characters, then it is also true that we can embody in our lives the artfulness with which those stories are told. We can go about living our lives in ways that help others become aware of the dense, enduring goodness in which we are graced to live, and move, and have our being. We can live lives fully realized in the giving and receiving of gifts rather than in the offering of sacrifices.

Dying the Same

But that cannot be the last word. As I am writing these words, I am learning about the murder of George Floyd. A white Minneapolis police officer, in the process of an arrest, which itself at this point seems questionable, forced the handcuffed Black man down on his face in the street and pressed his knee against his neck, holding him there in spite of his protests and the complaints of others standing on the sidewalk. "I can't breathe." Floyd says it over and over again, echoing Eric Garner's words. Someone is overheard saying something about a friend who died, and Floyd says, "I'm about to die the same." He says he cannot feel his face. Then, he loses consciousness and never regains it.

Obviously, there is no short, straight line to be drawn from this murder to our liturgies and liturgical art. But they are related, nonetheless, because our consciences—our very consciousness—is shaped by the sacrificial rather than the gracious. As Willie Jennings has said, "We repeat the mistake continuously in this country of trying to address our racial animus and the violence it fosters as though it were a virus that occasionally attacks our social body, rather than seeing the truth: that racial animus is a constituting reality of our social body." America was shaped from the ground up by a Christianity that had already accepted the lie of racism, a lie which grew from the forgetting of gentleness and the chosenness of Israel.[21] Therefore, Christianity in America was shaped from the ground up by a racism that justified itself in the language of election and sacrifice—not sacrifices offered so much as sacrifices required.

Toni Morrison's *Beloved*, like the Akedah, is a story about a family defined by a sacrifice. And it is a story that exposes how the American way of life is determined by the sacrifices we have forced others to make. The novel tells the story of Sethe, a former slave, whose back is covered with scars left by her master's whip. She refers to these scars as her "tree." Morrison's story is inspired by the account of Margaret Garner, a young, pregnant slave from Kentucky who escaped across the frozen Ohio River with her children and her husband, Robert Garner, in late January 1856. They had hoped to make their way through Cincinnati to Canada via the Underground Railroad, but her master, who was likely also the father of three of her children, found them. And he, along with the U.S. Marshals, surrounded the house where the Garners had been hiding. When Robert refused to surrender, the Marshals stormed the house, and rather than allowing her family to be taken into slavery, Margaret slit the throat of her two-year-old daughter, Mary, and stabbed herself and her other three children.

Roughly halfway through the novel, Sethe's secret is revealed. Four horsemen arrive at the house where she and her children are hiding: schoolteacher, her former master, and three others—"one nephew, one slave catcher and a sheriff." And they realize, slowly, that Sethe has run from the house with her children and hidden in a shed.

> Inside, two boys bled in the sawdust and dirt at the feet of a nigger woman holding a blood-soaked child to her chest with one hand and an infant by the heels in the other. She did not look at them; she simply swung the baby toward the wall planks, missed and tried to connect a second time, when out of nowhere—in the ticking time the men spent staring at what there was to stare—the old nigger boy, still mewing, ran through the door behind them and snatched the baby from the arch of its mother's swing.[22]

Late in the novel, Denver, Sethe's daughter—named for a white woman who saved Sethe's life while she was pregnant—realizes that her mother has been trying all her life to "make up for the handsaw." But, overhearing her mother talk to the ghost, she realizes too why Sethe had done it in the first place: it was the only act of love left. The only way to protect her daughter from a life worse than death. It was a sacrifice she was required to make.

> Anybody white could take your whole self for anything that came to mind. Not just work, kill, or maim you, but dirty you. Dirty you so bad you couldn't like yourself anymore. Dirty you so bad you forgot who you were and couldn't think it up. And though she and others lived through and got over it, she could never let it happen to her own. The best thing she was, was her children. Whites might dirty *her* all right, but not her best thing, her beautiful, magical best thing—the part of her that was clean.[23]

Morrison's story, like the story of Margaret Garner, like the story of Abraham and Isaac, is a story that must be passed on precisely because it is not a story to pass on. It allows us to see that our lives are backgrounded not only by God and not only by the unknown mysteries of nature that embrace our lives, but also by a history filled, if not defined, by unspeakable cruelties. Just so, it makes it possible for us to see that history for what it is, and to begin to do what we can to make restitution for it. We can do that only if we learn, finally, what Jesus and all of Israel's prophets have told us all along we have to come to understand: we can do justice only after we realize, down in our bones, that God hates, and has always hated, our sacrifices—especially those we have demanded from others. What he wants, all he wants, is *mercy*—the very mercy he tried to offer us as we made a sacrifice of him.

5

Beauty Will Not Save the World

Lent

There's no such thing as a Catholic novel, unless it's a piece of propaganda.
Muriel Spark

Merciful one, save me from slight repentance.
Anya Krugovoy Silver

Beauty is vain.
Proverbs 31:30

Lent and the Light of the Darkness

In a sermon for the first Sunday in Lent, Maggie Ross, the Anglican anchorite, exults in the "clean desert wind" of the Lenten season, mourning what popular Christianity has made of the practice of penitence. She worries that we have been conditioned to observe Lent by denigrating ourselves and punishing our bodies when, in truth, Lent is only parenthetically about sin and not at all about punishment. It is a time for recommitting ourselves to "beholding God," seeing ourselves and all things in the light of his devotion to us.[1] The good news, in other words, is good in part because it strips away our disillusions. Seeing God in the face of the dead Christ, we can begin to reckon with the fact that nothing is as it should be. We have been alienated from our own beauty.[2]

Beauty is estranged from itself. And that allows us to admit, without despair, that no beauty, not even God's beauty, can save our world—at least not in the way we want it to be saved.

Of course, there *are* ways in which it is right for us to say beauty saves the world. John Paul II, for example, argues in a letter to artists that "epiphanies of beauty" awaken in us the passion for life we need to overcome the troubles thrown up against us in this world.[3] And Aleksandr Solzhenitsyn contends that the beautiful possesses a "secret inner light," and when that light shines forth, the truth becomes undeniable and indisputable: "The convincingness of a true work of art is completely irrefutable and it forces even an opposing heart to surrender," and "falsehood can hold out against much in this world, but not against art."[4] Along similar lines, Paul Evdokimov says the graced beauty of the icon and the saint "introduces God into the soul like the burning bush whose roots go down deep into that same Beauty." And in this sense, he believes, the claim that beauty will save the world is justified.[5]

It is true: the beautiful does indeed trouble and enthuse us, reminding us both that the world needs to be saved and that it is worth saving. And it can, at least at times, open us up to the mysterious, bearing witness to the infinite generativity of God, freeing us to move, if always only haltingly, toward the holy, providing us "an obscure and ill-assured beginning of the knowledge of God."[6] Nonetheless, without giving in to bitterness or desolation, we have to accept the fact that no beauty, however glorious, however excellent, can keep us or our world from our fate. This is the hard word of the cross: beauty is vain (Prov 31:30), and all things, including the work of God in the world, have been subjected to futility (Rom 8:20). The hope we have, therefore, is a hope not in the beautiful but for it. Beauty cannot redeem. But it can be redeemed.

Elaine Scarry has recently and rightly defended the beautiful against old and new suspicions, championing its power to prepare us for the work of justice, celebrating, as Pope John Paul II did, the ways beauty restores our "aliveness," awakening our sense of fairness, fitness, and proportionality without which we cannot make sound judgments. She rightly reminds us that the beautiful sometimes summons us to act, "to bring new beauty into the world," and in this way "brings us face-to-face with our own powers to create," the very powers which we must draw on if we hope to overcome the many injustices that imperil the common good and our shared well-being.[7] Still, her work does not fully acknowledge beauty's inherent ambiguity and essential conflictedness. As a result, it by and large fails to account for why it is that beauty is so rarely effectual and how it is that beauty is so often and so easily instrumentalized for appalling, despicable ends.[8]

And that reality brings us up hard against the truth: whatever we might want to believe, our cultural achievements and aesthetic sophistications do not deliver us from the evils at work without or within us. In the same way, the experience of the beautiful does not in and of itself cure our viciousness or secure us against the brutality of existence. Indeed, as George Steiner says, "bookishness, highest literacy, every technique of cultural propaganda and training, not only can accompany bestiality and oppression and despotism but at certain points foster it."[9] To put it bluntly, then, beauty does not always beautify, is not always good for us, and does not always press or draw us toward the truth. And this is so not only because we fail to see its radiance or resist its graces, but also because beauty is estranged from itself just as we are estranged from ourselves. Ours is a fallen and gone-wrong world, a world subjected to futility and fated for extinction. The beautiful can and very often does "go wildly wrong,"[10] and we are, as the prayer book says, wretched (Rom 7:24).[11]

Loveliness in the Time of Cholera

The Christian tradition warns against the dangers of beauty at every turn—the beauty of the city, the beauty of music, the beauty of thought, the beauty of words, the beauty of the body. Gregory of Nyssa, for example, in his *Life of Macrina*, celebrates his sister's victory over her own attractiveness, a victory which she achieves only as she is dying, her lovely body at last one with the loveliness of God. As Natalie Carnes explains, in Gregory's telling Macrina's loveliness remains treacherous until it is finally fully transfigured into a sign of God's purity:

> While it was always a sign of divine presence for one such as Gregory, who had eyes to see it, it is now a sign of divine presence for everyone. As such, it is no longer dangerous in the sense of tempting sexual response. Her body points to God. Even the once-cancerous breast that was hidden from doctors is laid bare for Gregory, also a sign of God's grace.[12]

To be sure, Gregory did not think Macrina deserved blame for being desirable. He knew the danger had to do entirely with the lusts of men around her and the violence inherent in the society in which she was forced to live. Nonetheless, his argument is clear: Macrina is to be praised for overcoming her desirability and for striving at every turn to free herself from her womanly nature. And not only that: what is true of her body is also true of her words, as well as his own. Words can and should be excellent, but that excellence remains fraught with danger. This holds true even when speaking of Scripture. Gregory finds the Psalms, in particular, perfectly beautiful. And yet, he knows not all who read the Psalms are made beautiful.[13] Thus, for Gregory, the beautiful is beautifying only as it is given and received rightly, and never used to satisfy selfish ambitions or wanton desires.

St. Augustine, in what is perhaps his best-known letter, makes a similar argument, instructing the widowed Proba to consider herself desolate no matter what happens to her: "This is indeed a dying life, whatever mortal comfort it may shower on us, whatever companions may share it with us, whatever wealth of worldly goods it may lavish on us."[14] And in his *Ascent of Mount Carmel*, a work which is itself nothing if not perilously beautiful, St. John of the Cross observes, almost offhandedly, that many who seek perfection in the spiritual life sometimes beg God to strip them of their graces, disfiguring them so they are repulsive to themselves and thus desirable for God. He does not call his readers to pray this prayer. But he does press them to hold their natural graces lightly, and he condemns excessive attachment in the fiercest terms: "a person attached to the beauty of any creature is extremely ugly in God's sight."[15] It is this line of thinking that shows itself in Evdokimov's understanding of the icon. Iconographers, he argues, must strive to avoid artistic overstatement, because an icon is truly an icon—and not merely a painting—only when it is not in and of itself spectacular, only when it draws no attention to itself at all as a work of art but "simply lets true beauty shine forth."[16]

No doubt, these ancient and medieval Christian anxieties are shot through with misogynistic and misanthropic presumptions and impulses.[17] Even so, it would be a mistake to dismiss them out of hand. Carnes argues that a mother's love, natural as it may be, can be corroded by a false self-image and a self-serving desire to be for her child more than she ought to be.[18] And the same is true of all of our relationships, including the most intimate and most life-giving. We are plagued by the gone-wrongness of the world; therefore, what is true of love and lovers in Gabriel García Márquez' *Love in the Time of Cholera* is also true of loveliness itself and our relation to it.[19] Márquez' novel ends with erstwhile lovers, Florentino and Fermina, together at last, giving and receiving long-needed kindnesses. Uncareful readers invariably come away convinced they have read an old-fashioned if somewhat unconventional romance. But in truth *Love in the Time of Cholera* is an indictment of our scandalous gullibility and a startling reminder that love and loveliness not only cannot keep us from our fate but also are themselves diseased and deepen our trouble. Whatever we tell ourselves, the voyage cannot last forever.[20]

God Makes Nothing but Riddles

"Beauty will save the world": it is common knowledge that this statement comes from Dostoevsky's *The Idiot*. But in fact, Myshkin never says it outright. The consumptive and suicidal Ippolit, Myshkin's nihilistic double, asks the prince in a frenzy if he did in fact once make the claim. But before Myshkin can answer, Ippolit dismisses his response: "The prince says that the world will be saved by beauty! But I say that he has such whimsical notions merely because he's presently in love." The prince blushes, and Ippolit continues to mock him: "What sort of beauty will save the world? Kolya told me about it . . . Are you a zealous Christian? Kolya said you call yourself a Christian."[21]

Myshkin is, in fact, in love—with two women. He falls first for Nastasya Filippovna, "the most beautiful woman in St. Petersburg," only having seen her portrait. Afterward, he falls for Aglaya, the youngest Yepanchin sister. Nastasya's beauty, we are told, is "dazzling" and "strange," "ravishing" and "positively unendurable."[22] Aglaya's loveliness is also devastating; Myshkin admits he is afraid even to look at her. When her mother presses him, he demurs: "Beauty is difficult to judge; I'm not ready yet. Beauty is a riddle."[23] His words are reminiscent of another of Dostoevsky's characters: "Beauty is a terrible and frightening thing. It is terrible because it has not been fathomed, and can't be fathomed, for God makes nothing but riddles."[24]

During Myshkin's initial visit to the Yepanchin estate immediately after his arrival in St. Petersburg, he sees Nastasya's photograph for the first time and is entranced by her—not by desire so much as by something more like pity. "Her face is cheerful, but she has suffered dreadfully, don't you think? Her eyes betray it . . . It's a proud face, a dreadfully proud one, and I simply can't tell if she is good or not. Oh, if only she were good! It would redeem everything!"[25] Lizaveta Prokofyevna, General Yepanchin's wife and the prince's distant relative, takes the portrait from him and considers it for herself:

> "So that's the sort of beauty you like?" she said, turning to the prince suddenly. "Yes . . . that sort . . ." the prince replied with a certain effort. "You mean precisely that sort?" "Precisely that sort." "Why?" "In that face . . . there is much suffering . . ." the prince said quietly, almost involuntarily, as though he were talking to himself, and not answering a question.[26]

Adelaida, one of Aglaya's older sisters, sees the portrait and gasps in shock: "Beauty like that is power . . . With beauty like that one may turn the world upside down!"[27] In fact, as the story unfolds, Nastasya does indeed wreck the lives of those who love her. And by the end, all of their lives are in ruins.

In Michael Powell's and Emeric Pressberger's *Black Narcissus*, a small mission of Anglican nuns labors to establish a Christian presence amongst the Hindus high in the Himalayas. The nuns take up residence in a magnificent, abandoned palace on a towering cliff at the invitation of the local raja, once the home of his harem. Starting a school and a hospital for the care of the locals, they go about their work with zeal. But they are pressed more and more by unaccountable glories, natural and unnatural. And, in the end, their faith and their sanity crack under the amassing weight. As Wendy Brenner, in a dazzling essay, explains,

> The escalating hallucinogenic beauty of the remote, half-ruined Himalayan palace to which the British nuns are sent drives each of them slowly mad in her own way. One secretly mail-orders a bright red dress and lipstick from the city, another is haunted by relentless memories of an emerald necklace and earrings she gave up years ago, and the no-nonsense sister in charge of the garden finds herself surreptitiously planting beds of exotic flowers instead of the vegetables they all need to survive. *There is no escape from beauty*, the film seems to say.[28]

The Idiot tells more or less the same story. But when all is said and done, it is Myshkin's beauty, even more than Nastasya's or Aglaya's, that proves to be too much. Berdyaev suggests that the idiot eventually loses himself in "the gulf of his own pity." But it would be nearer the truth to say he is from first to last nothing but that gulf: others are swallowed up by him. To be fair, he is not entirely to blame for his own faults and failures, not any more than Nastasya or Rogozhin are to blame for theirs. He happens to be the occasion, if not exactly the cause, of the tragedy that befalls those whom he loves. But he is far more dangerous than they are, precisely because he is better than they are. He is, in Berdyaev's words, "seraphic," loving wholeheartedly but "without flesh and blood." And just for that reason, he cannot endure the world and the world cannot endure him.[29] Maritain, in a famous line, glories in the fact that "infinity wounds the finite" through that "certain sacred weakness" that appears in the flaws and lacks in our lives and in our art.[30] But Myshkin's weakness is absolute, and so can neither truly bless nor hallow. It does not wound: it obliterates. He is beautiful, but his beauty is inescapably destructive. And he cannot escape himself.

The Wholly Beautiful Man

In a January 1868 letter to a friend, Dostoevsky shared his hopes to write the story of "the wholly beautiful man."[31] And in his notebooks, he refers to Myshkin as "Prince Christ."[32] Not without reason, then, readers have often taken Myshkin as a Christ figure. Herman Hesse, for example, remarks that he is exhausted with the constant likening of Myshkin to Jesus, but admits that Dostoevsky's "idiot," like Jesus, is "touched" and characterized by a uniquely perilous innocence:

> What is it that makes this "idiot" so impossible in the world of other people? Why does no one understand him, even though almost all love him in some fashion, almost everyone finds his gentleness sympathetic, indeed often exemplary? What distinguishes him, the man of magic, from the others, the ordinary people? Why are they right in rejecting him? Why must they do it, inevitably? Why must things go with him as they did with Jesus, who in the end was abandoned not only by the world but by all his disciples as well?[33]

The prince's incorruptibility proves to be dangerous for others, too. "He is understood by criminals and by hysterics; he, the innocent, the gentle child! But this child, by God, is not as gentle as he seems. His innocence is by no means harmless, and people quite properly fear him." Edward Wasiolek, in his introduction to Dostoevsky's notebooks, grants that the Idiot is "ineffectual," leaving the world no better and perhaps even worse than he found it. He grants too that Myshkin's presence imposes an unbearable burden on others. But he insists that the prince, like Christ, "was not meant to quiet the world, but to threaten it." And even if he failed to transform it through his threats that is no proof of failure. After all, "if we were to measure Christ by pragmatic results, he too might appear to be an emissary of darkness rather than of light."[34] Wasiolek no doubt has a point: Christ did not bring about the change his disciples expected, or that we want to see. But it would be a mistake to conclude that we are left only with tragedy. In fact, as David Bentley Hart contends, the tragic is precisely what the story of Jesus exposes as a lie—even if it is sometimes the most beautiful lie.[35]

Ironically, it is only when we have accepted that Christ's death does not save us or our world from dying that we can understand what it means to have been promised the restoration of all things. The empty tomb is not the sign of a happy ending, but a sign that even the most tragic ending is not self-determining and self-interpreting. We have been promised the setting-right of all that has happened in our gone-wrong world, and that is infinitely better than the restoration of some moral balance. Lent reminds us that we can come to hope in that restoration only on the far side of holy disillusionment. Maggie Smith is right: we should try to sell our children the world:

> Any decent realtor,
> walking you through a real shithole, chirps on
> about good bones: This place could be beautiful,
> right? You could make this place beautiful.[36]

But even if we are more or less successful, these bones will break, too, eventually. We build our houses in vain, even if we do it under God's care. And the Christian life ends no differently than other lives end. Even so, as we "go the way of all the earth," we can "live small," enjoying the good life gives us, give thanks for all God's gifts, and wonder at the wildness of it all.[37] And what is true of us, personally, is true of our communities, our species, our planet, our cosmos. But this does not shake our confidence, because we know that the whole creation, precisely to be itself, must be conformed to the image of Christ—becoming like him in his death and in that way attaining resurrection from the dead.

Lent and the Body of the Dead Christ

During his manic "necessary explanation," which he admits was written in a fit of near madness, Ippolit describes the experience of seeing a copy of Hans Holbein's *The Body of the Dead Christ in the Tomb* for the first time, an experience he says that did not register until he had returned home in a state of delirium. Then, it came back to him in fragments. The painting lacked "artistic merit." And yet, it left a deep impression, he realized, because all the other paintings of Christ he had seen depicted the savior as noble and self-possessed even in his worst sufferings. Holbein's painting, however, portrayed the unstinted horror and severity of death—God's death. Ippolit knows that Christians believe Jesus truly suffered and died. Still, he cannot imagine how anyone who saw the dead Jesus could recover from the sight. If even this man dies, after having lived the life he lived, how could anyone ever again doubt the supremacy of death? Those who saw Christ in that state, he concludes, must have gone away with a consciousness of death and its power that not even Christ's resurrection could drive out of them.[38]

When Myshkin notices the painting in Rogozhin's house, he gives it only a fleeting glance, merely registering that it is a reproduction of the younger Holbein's famous painting. He speaks of it as little more than a curiosity. But after Rogozhin claims to like looking at it, the prince suddenly senses a danger: "Some people might lose their faith by looking at their painting!"[39] Later, for reasons he does not try to understand, the prince finds himself thinking again of the painting and its strange effects on his friend.[40] But even in this moment, he seems not so much frightened as oddly unsettled. In fact, he never seems to feel truly, personally at risk in the presence of the image of the dead Christ. As he more or less admitted in his remark to Rogozhin, *someone* might lose faith—but he would not. It is precisely this innocence that makes him dangerous. As Williams observes, "Myshkin is a 'good' person who cannot avoid doing harm." He cannot or at least will not decide for or against anyone or anything, and so he becomes "unwittingly a force of destruction." He makes "no adult choices." And as a result, he cannot mature or flourish or help others toward fullness and flourishing. He exists as "a man with no history." And the effects of his innocence are fatal.[41] Diane Thompson makes the point sharply:

> Myshkin resolves into a tragic parody of Christ, a failed kenosis without the backbone of the Word. The Idiot moves us by the tragic spectacle of goodness defeated, of innocence corrupted, of a great promise come to naught. Myshkin sinks into permanent darkness, bereft of speech, as impotent in the living death of his incurable idiocy as the Christ of Holbein's painting.[42]

By this account, the prince's innocence is nothing but a shadow of Christ's holiness, and unlike Peter, whose shadow would fall on the sick and heal them (Acts 5:15), Myshkin leaves only darkness in his wake.

In his Dostoevsky book, Williams describes Holbein's painting as an "anti-icon," arguing that according to classical Orthodox iconography, the icon always necessarily confronts worshippers with the direct gaze of Christ (or his Mother or the saints). Only demons, and sometimes Judas Iscariot, are shown in profile. Thus, to depict Christ not alive but dead, and not standing or sitting face-front but lying prone and in profile, is "a double negation of the iconographic convention." Holbein's painting, then, at least in Williams' estimation, is a "diabolical" image, presenting only a "nonpresence," one which mirrors Myshkin's own deadly character.[43] But other readings of the painting and its relation to Myshkin remain possible. Perhaps Holbein's image is not diabolical but prophetic, revealing that Christ's life-giving presence cannot be negated even by death? Understood in this way, the painting mirrors Myshkin's character only in the sense that it shows the irreversible contrast between the prince's innocence and Christ's holiness. Myshkin, in fact, *is* a good person, in a sense even "unfallen." But because of his own goodness, he cannot keep from devastating those around him. Christ, however, assumes even these failures, claiming them as his own.[44] The prince's kenosis fails abysmally, no doubt. But if the gospel is to be trusted, then Christ's self-offering extends even to those depths. Therefore, whatever Dostoevsky might have intended, Holbein's *The Body of the Dead Christ in the Tomb*, as well as Myshkin's and Rogozhin's and Ippolit's responses to it, need not be taken to mean that Christ's intercession is necessarily tragic. Instead, they can be read as a witness to the truth that Christ's intercession assumes the tragic outcomes of our wretched existence without in any way being debased by it, breaking it once for all in his own brokenness. Our existence, at least as we know it now, is tragic. But it cannot touch the depths of the life of God.

Cormac McCarthy's *The Road* ends with a devastatingly beautiful coda:

> Once there were brook trout in the streams in the mountains. You could see them standing in the amber current where the white edges of their fins wimpled softly in the flow. They smelled of moss in your hand. Polished and muscular and torsional. On their backs were vermiculate patterns that were maps of the world in its becoming. Maps and mazes. Of a thing which could not be put back. Not be made right again. In the deep glens where they lived all things were older than man and they hummed of mystery.[45]

McCarthy's canticle may seem to contradict Christian hope. But in truth it gives voice to it. It contradicts historical optimism and the ideals of "progress." McCarthy knows that history does not arc toward wholeness but simply unwinds to nothing. History is, as Tolkien said, "a long defeat." And this is good news, in spite of everything. We have to face the fact, as Abraham did, that we and everyone and everything we love are already as good as dead (Rom 4:19). We have to know we will not be kept from death, but that after death has swallowed us up, we shall be raised from the dead and in that way death itself shall be destroyed. Only in the end, which comes not in time as its finale but happens to it as its transfiguration, can we taunt our enemy: "Where, O death, is your victory? Where, O death, is your sting?" (1 Cor 15:55).

"There can be no redemption without beauty's descent into hell."[46] But even that is not enough to save us. There can be no redemption without the death of beauty in hell. And that is exactly what God has achieved and suffered in Christ. The wholly beautiful man, the altogether lovely one, descended into hell—and he did not survive. But God, against all hope, raised him from the dead—and that means the death of death and the damnation of hell. As Holbein's painting shows, the body of the dead Christ, disfigured by evil and its corruptions, has no remaining beauty. But his corpse reveals more than that the world cannot be saved from death and that all things must die, including all that has been made beautiful in God's time. It reveals that we are not left hopeless because Jesus is the one who died and was raised as the beginning of a new creation. That is the mystery that hums even now in all things.

Standing before Holbein's painting, the young Myshkin seems inexplicably, clumsily naive, idiotically indifferent to what has happened to Jesus and what will happen to him. Ippolit, by contrast, seems spellbound, almost mystically caught up in horror, forgetting that it is Christ who is dead. Their responses, taken together, make plain the need for Lenten disillusionment. We have to die to beauty before we can receive it truthfully, in ways that are actually good for us. And so, the one who claims, or at least wants to believe, that beauty will save the world must come up hard against the truth that beauty, given or made, must be saved from itself and from us and so for us. Beauty will not save the world. But it is precisely that world which cannot be saved and that beauty which fails to save the world that God has promised to redeem. Only the world that cannot be saved will be saved. And only the beauty that cannot save the world is worth saving after all.

6

A Most Unspectacular Passion

Good Friday

Jesus established nothing, founded nothing, achieved nothing.
He did not transform the world ... The Father has not accomplished his will through any success of Jesus; Jesus is left with
nothing but his love and his obedience, and this is the prayer
to the Father to work through his failure.

Herbert McCabe

We have become a spectacle to the world.

1 Corinthians 4:9

Beauty can be a great threat. Beauty frightens.

Clarice Lispector

An Artist's Passion

Mel Gibson's *The Passion of the Christ* (2004) was by all accounts
a landmark film and a huge box office success. But it proved to be
incredibly polarizing even before it premiered. Months before its
2004 Ash Wednesday release, a group of academics that included
New Testament scholars Paula Fredriksen and Amy-Jill Levine
condemned the script, warning that if it was not seriously revised
the film would stir up deep-seated anti-Semitic prejudices and
do grave harm to the Jewish community. At the same time, many
leading evangelicals, including Billy Graham, Joel Osteen, Rick
Warren, Pat Robertson, and Jerry Falwell, endorsed the film. A
few Jewish conservative leaders did, as well. Rabbi Daniel Lapin,
for example, predicted *The Passion* would spark "America's third

great religious reawakening.["]1 Unsurprisingly, many conservative Catholics also defended it. And in December, a couple of months before its debut, a *Wall Street Journal* column reported that Pope John Paul II had seen the film and had said, simply: "It is as it was."2 Later, the Vatican denied the report, and in January a spokesperson issued an official statement saying the Holy Father had indeed seen the film but would refrain from giving a public opinion on it or any other work of art.3

Needless to say, critics were divided by the film, too. Roger Ebert praised it, as did James Berardinelli, Peter Travers, and Richard Corliss. But they all also acknowledged its unnerving violence. Ebert said, flatly, "This is the most violent film I have ever seen."4 More than a few reviews condemned it as "torture porn" or "snuff." In his *New Yorker* post, David Denby named it a "sickening death trip, a grimly unilluminating procession of treachery, beatings, blood, and agony." And he said he was concerned not only about its portrayal of Jews, but also its impact on Christians: "How, I wonder, will people become better Christians if they are filled with the guilt, anguish, or loathing that this movie may create in their souls?"5 Mark Kermode called it "an exploitation film par excellence" and "an anguished howl," suggesting it did not tell the story of Jesus so much as lay bare Gibson's own tortured soul.6

In the immediate aftermath, a number of Christian scholars denounced *The Passion* as unhistorical and hateful, and an affront to the gospel. Ched Myers, for example, criticized Gibson's decision to portray the Jewish high priest, Caiaphas, as irrationally cruel and in league with the devil, while humanizing Pilate, the Roman procurator. And he also criticized Gibson's decision to tell the story of Jesus' death without attending to the teaching and miracles that provoked Roman and Jewish leaders to arrest Jesus and execute him. In Myers' view, Gibson's choices effectively reaffirmed two of Christendom's darkest legacies: scapegoating Jews and naively regarding imperial authority as inherently good and beneficial.7

Other scholars put forward more or less substantive apologies for the film. Mark Goodacre, for example, a professor of religion at Duke University and an expert on the origins of Christianity, defended it, although primarily on cinematic, not biblical or historical grounds. To counter the charges of anti-Semitism, he pointed to the casting of Maia Morgenstern, a devout Jew whose father survived the Holocaust, as Jesus' mother, and to the rewriting of the story of Simon of Cyrene as a Jew who intercedes to defend Jesus against Roman brutality. Goodacre argued, too, that Gibson's *Passion* is not nearly as violent as many have claimed, submitting that overreaction to the movie's supposed failings obscured its most remarkable aspects, including the audacious choice to show so much of what happens from Jesus' own point of view.[8]

Along different lines, Columbia professor and Kierkegaard scholar Mark Taylor theorized that in spite of what the critics themselves claimed, most criticisms of *The Passion* actually took offense not at the violence as such, but at the underlying Christian beliefs about the meaning of that violence: "the culmination of the Incarnation is the Crucifixion, in which God's flesh and blood are radically confirmed. If flesh does not bleed, it is not real, and if flesh is not real, there is no Incarnation." Taylor cited a controversial 1986 article in the *Journal of the American Medical Association*, which offered a "careful and vivid description of the method and physiology of crucifixion as the Romans practiced it around the time Jesus is supposed to have died," and explained that in his view the reactions to the article, like the reactions to Gibson's film, betray the fact that the postmodern West is scandalized by Christian convictions about the nature of flesh—in particular, the wounded flesh of the tortured Jesus.[9]

Surely the most unlikely champion of *The Passion* was René Girard, famous for his work on the uses of scapegoating and violence to maintain social order. But in an article that coincided with the release of the film in France, Girard did in fact defend it, maintaining that in spite of what many had said about it in the press, the film was by and large true to the Gospels, and anything but anti-Semitic. Even more surprisingly, Girard argued that its vivid depictions of Christ's sufferings, far from being pornographic, actually served to expose the deep injustices and delusions of mimetic violence, thus pointing the way toward a more peaceful future. He argued that there are essentially only two attitudes toward violence in human history: the mythological, which seeks to "cover the nudity of human violence with Noah's cloak," and the realistic, which dares to face the innocence of victims, and heroically places truth over even the social order. Gibson's *Passion*, in his estimation, "makes every effort to be faithful" to this latter attitude.[10]

Realism and Reality

At the heart of Girard's apology is a commitment to an inchoate theory of realism. He admits that the Gospels refer to the cruelties Christ suffered without even attempting to describe them in detail, without in any way "making us see the Passion 'as if we were there.'" But he insists that is only because in the ancient world realistic representation was imaginatively impossible. He postulates, too, that it was Christian reflection on Jesus' death that eventually led to the invention of realism. In his view, then, *The Passion of the Christ* fulfills the artistic impulse latent in the Gospel accounts, and precisely so restores to the crucifixion its "scandalous force."

> The writers of the Gospels did not deliberately reject a possibility that did not exist during their era. It is clear that far from fleeing realism, they seek to create it, but the means are lacking. The narratives of the Passion contain more concrete details than all of the learned works of the time. They represent a first step in the direction of the ever-increasing realism that defines the essential dynamism of our culture in its periods of great vitality. The first impulse of realism is the desire to strengthen religious meditation, which is essentially a meditation on the Passion of Christ.[11]

As we have seen, Taylor suggested that many critics loathed the film because of its depiction of "flesh." He also argued, however, that many loved it because they were consumed by the post-modern thirst for "realism," a desire which is bound up with a literalism that leads inevitably to violence of all kinds, artistic and political. "When reality becomes image, there is a longing for blood, even if it is on celluloid. It is much easier to divide the world between good guys and bad guys when you think you know the literal truth. Literalism and some form of Manichaeism, in other words, are inseparable."[12] Girard takes more or less the opposite standpoint: only "implacable realism" can overcome the need for violence.

At one point, Girard suggests that cinema is in some sense a perfection of Christian witness, surpassing other art forms, including the paintings of Caravaggio, Bosch, and Mantegna, "extending and surpassing the techniques of great literary and pictorial realism." The nature of cinema requires that "these horrific things must be represented 'as if we were there.'"[13] It is not entirely clear, however, what he means by "realism" and even less clear that it is the right way to talk about Gibson's film. In everyday speech, we refer to paintings as "realistic" when they seem plain and unstylized. We imagine that the less "artistic" they are, the more they show us life "as it is." For the same reason, we regard candid photographs and raw video footage as almost perfectly natural, and so truthful in ways art cannot be. But Gibson's *Passion* is obviously, unmistakably stylized, both narratively and cinematically. There is nothing natural about it. The script, which Gibson cowrote, is an original work, weaving together a single new version of the last hours of Christ's life from various strands of the four Gospels, as well as Catholic devotional literature. And his direction is also anything but plain: think, for example, of his use of slow motion, the ludicrously oversize cross Jesus is forced to carry, the painterly scene of Mary holding the dead body of her son, the divine teardrop. So, whatever we make of Girard's theorizing about realism, *The Passion of the Christ* is not a plain retelling of the events of Good Friday just as they happened and just as they are storied in the Gospels. But even if it had been, it still could not have reproduced anything like the experience of "being there." It is not as it was, and can never be, no matter the form of art. So-called realistic images or films do not bring us closer to the reality of what those who were there then actually experienced. Even startlingly lifelike works do not tell the truth more truly. Caravaggio's *The Incredulity of Saint Thomas*, for example, is not truer than, say, a Byzantine icon of the saint or John's Gospel's characterizing of him. And if it were possible, a photograph of Thomas would not be truer than either the painting or the icon or the biblical narrative. All to say, then, even if Girard had been right to say that Gibson's film is "realistic," what he infers from it is profoundly mistaken. The Gospel is not more faithfully told in "realistic" representation. In fact, more often than not reality is lost altogether in the "realism." Besides, in Christian thought the purpose of art is to attune us to reality as it comes to us in all of its furtive complexity, to open our eyes and ears, to teach us attentiveness, not to reproduce for us the experience of another's reality we wish to make our own. And given that Christians believe that Jesus is God living a fully human life, they hold that his experience is radically other than ours. His experience is unique and primary, real in a way that makes reality what it is. So, neither art nor nature can do any more than bear weak and disjointed witness to it.

Realism and Sentimentality

In spite of Goodacre's dismissals, *The Passion of the Christ* is unbearably violent. But it is not the violence per se that is most disturbing: it is the characterization of those who do the violence. The devil appears only a few times; the devilish appears everywhere, however, as do the maniacal and the surreal. Before Jesus is flogged, the Roman soldiers bark and hiss and cackle. Moments later, as they beat and whip Jesus mercilessly, they are enraptured and euphoric, intoxicated by the pain they are inflicting on him and on those who are watching. Of course, the viewer cannot bear to see or hear this horror, and so instinctively looks away and covers her ears, just as do Jesus' mother and John and Mary Magdalene. But Caiaphas and most of the other high priests show no such pity, and the androgynous Satan, clutching a monstrous infant, slithers among them—a sure sign that they are filled with his evil. Afterward, when Jesus is led back to the governor's palace, Pilate sees his sickening wounds and grimaces, obviously moved by compassion. But Caiaphas, seeing his wounds, does not so much as flinch. Instead, he screams, and the mob joins him, chanting: "Crucify him!"

Jeremy Begbie has warned against sentimentality in art, which he describes as the self-indulgent misrepresentation of reality through the elision or trivializing of evil.[14] By that definition, *The Passion of the Christ* is an example of *anti*-sentimentality: the self-indulgent misrepresentation of reality through the *exaggeration* of evil. Hence, in spite of what Taylor suggests, the film's offensiveness is not so much in its portrayal of the flesh of Jesus but in its senseless brutalizing of his body and the dehumanizing of those who brutalize him. It is one thing to show that Jesus is savaged. It is an altogether different thing to show his enemies as savages. Not only because such offensive portrayals call up anti-Semitic propaganda, which Christians have used against Jews for centuries, but also because they obscure the fact that monstrous evils are almost always done not by monsters, but by ordinary people, often with the best intentions and with the clearest consciences.

One of the most breathlessly laudatory reviews of *The Passion* described it as "a miracle, a gift of God . . . the most realistic and spectacular portrayal of Christ ever to have been realized on film," and declared that it "presents the Good News in a way that has never been more compelling since the original." The praise did not stop there: "Rather than watching an actor attempting to portray Christ, it was as if we were watching an old friend suffer for us. Jim Caviezel's portrayal of Jesus is by far the deepest and most convincing to date—restrained, yet surprisingly rich in meaning, and rendered with a dignity that can only be communicated by an actor who is, in some mysterious way, living through the story in communion with its central character." But above and beyond these acclamations, the reviewer found in the film what seemed to him a means of grace:

> Contrition for our sins is often hard to come by. It is difficult to comprehend that our sins have hurt Jesus. The Passion of the Christ bursts through this barrier. I felt sorrow and shed tears for my sins, not because I had been caught, not even because I feared the loss of heaven or the pains of hell, but most of all, because my sins were the scourges that inflicted such suffering on my Lord—the good God made flesh to save me from my sins, my brother, my Saviour, my king.[15]

It may seem bad form to criticize a testimony like this one. Many, no doubt, will take it as proof of the legitimacy of Gibson's film. Most of us have been taught that the power to awaken pious feeling is the surest mark of validity for any work of art. Girard suggests "realism" developed as an aid to devotional feeling. But surely that is not in itself a mark of validity: our affections say at least as much about us as they do about a work of art. Besides, at least some voices in the Christian tradition suggest that our devotional feelings need constantly to be brought into question.

In Salinger's *Catcher in the Rye*, Holden ends up at the movies. He hates the picture, predictably, and is seated next to a mother who cries throughout the movie, ignoring the increasingly desperate pleas of her son. "The phonier it got, the more she cried," he says. He admits that he would have thought that someone who cries at movies is "kindhearted." But this woman ignored her son's complaints, insisting that he should sit still and be quiet. Holden concludes, "She was about as kindhearted as a goddam wolf. You take somebody that cries their goddam eyes out over phony stuff in the movies, and nine times out of ten they're mean bastards at heart. I'm not kidding."[16]

Begbie is concerned precisely with this kind of pathological emotionalism, which he argues is inextricably bound up with cruelty: "The sentimentalist loves and hates, grieves or pities not for the sake of the other but for the sake of enjoying love, hate, grief or pity."[17] But *The Passion of the Christ* presents a different and more difficult problem, one that easily misleads even the discerning because it exaggerates evil and, in particular, the evil done to Jesus. Seeing a Christ figure suffer such unspeakable abuse, Christians cannot help but be deeply moved, because we feel we know him as our friend, our kin, our God. Still, the emotional response the film evokes is one-dimensional and self-indulgent. It is narcissistic, in spite of the fact that it focuses our eyes on another. It is narcissistic because we feel ourselves feeling what we think we should have always felt for Jesus, and so are elated that we feel it at last. As the reviewer said, contrition is "hard to come by."

Tellingly, in Gibson's *Passion*, Mary's and Judas' sufferings move us in ways Jesus' sufferings do not. Watching them, we sense something of the spiritual depths of their helplessness and hopelessness. But his sufferings, horrifying as they are, are overwhelmingly physical; so, they seem shallow and meaningless by comparison. In the end, then, Judas' wretchedness moves us to pity, and Mary's sorrow stirs up our compassion. But Jesus' woundedness either simply repulses us, or, worse, makes us seem repulsive to ourselves. And nothing is more vain or mean than false guilt.

Spectators and the Spectacle

Perhaps it is the job of "show business" to make the story of Jesus spectacular. No one would question that Gibson has done that. And perhaps some stories are rightly told spectacularly. But not the story of Good Friday. To make a spectacle of Jesus' death leaves us mere spectators, viewers and bystanders who cannot see Jesus for who he is or what is happening to him for what it is. Hence, what Jean-Louis Chrétien says about speech and song is equally true of cinema:

> When speech tries to unveil God instead of letting itself be unveiled and stripped bare, the loss of its dramatic tension

is also a loss of light and intelligibility. If there is a divine beauty, we cannot be its spectators, but only its witnesses. And the witnesses of such beauty speak in proportion to their wound and their sense of being torn apart . . . Song is existence only when it is wounded to the heart by what it sings, and breaks down, shattered by the radiance of what it sings—and yet still continues to sing.[18]

Ironically, and tragically, Gibson's "speech" is not at all wounded or torn apart. His camera is not a witness. Sometimes, it does not even settle for being a spectator, but instead assumes a false and safe transcendence, arrogating to itself the divine perspective, daring to show us what all this horror looks like from Christ's own point of view, or, even more troublingly, the Father's.

This runs counter both to truly Christian theology and truly Christian art, which alike are marked by the conflictedness of the cross and the ineffability of Christ's experiences. The medieval poet Jacopone da Todi, for example, breaks off in the middle of a hymn to own the impossibility of his praise:

> To speak of holy Love?
> Human speech cannot rise to such heights.
> In speaking of this love
> The tongues of angels falter–
> And you feel no misgivings and shame?
> You reduce love
> To the measure of your words;
> This is not praise, but blasphemy.[19]

John Donne's "Good Friday, 1613. Riding Westward" knows that the only way to move toward Christ is to turn away from him, because he is "that spectacle of too much weight for mee." The poet feels the threat of his vision. In words that recall the final lines of the *Paradiso*, he reflects on the impossibility of the creature understanding what it means for the creator to suffer a creaturely fate:

> Could I behold those hands which span the Poles,
> And tune all spheares at once peirc'd with those holes?
> Could I behold that endlesse height which is
> Zenith to us, and our Antipodes,
> Humbled below us? or that blood which is
> The seat of all our Soules, if not of his,
> Made durt of dust, or that flesh which was worne
> By God, for his apparell, rag'd, and torne?

It proves too much for him, and at last he can only beg:

> O Saviour, as thou hang'st upon the tree;
> I turne my backe to thee, but to receive
> Corrections, till thy mercies bid thee leave.
> O thinke mee worth thine anger, punish mee,
> Burne off my rusts, and my deformity,
> Restore thine Image, so much, by thy grace,
> That thou may'st know mee, and I'll turne my face.[20]

It is true, as Chrétien says, that "the beauty of Christ in the Passion is conveyed through its opposite."[21] And so, it only makes sense that we cannot speak of that beauty easily or cheaply. We must feel the risk: praise can so quickly turn to blasphemy, just as blasphemy can so quickly turn to praise. If, then, our speech or our craft is to be at all recognizably Christian, it cannot be slick or glib or crafty. Not that it has to be artless. But it must be marked by the pain of trying and failing to say what we feel needs to be said about the truth we know we are always only beginning to understand. What Jenson says of church architecture is true of all Christian art: we must never find it simply soothing.[22] Our hallelujahs must be broken. Or, to say the same thing another way, if we have no misgivings about our art, no hesitancy or trepidation in our speech, no shame about what we have failed to do and say, we can be sure that what we are making or saying is not in fact a gift. Precisely for these reasons, the story of Jesus' death cannot be made spectacular or sensational. That is a betrayal of its very essence. His story must be told in ways that suppress and defer, quell and revoke. His image, his loveliness, must be shown to have, in the words of the prophet, "no form or comeliness."

St. Augustine, once professor of rhetoric in Milan, knew this perfectly well. As Auerbach discerned in a landmark essay, Augustine's theology is as sensitive to the style of divine revelation as he is to its content. "Scripture is not always simple; it contains mysteries and hidden meaning; much of it seems obscure. But even the difficult ideas are not presented in a learned 'haughty' style that would intimidate and repel the simple man." Indeed, "there is no fundamental difference between the profound, obscure passages and those that are clear and simple." This formal modesty and self-effacement is essential, Augustine insists, because the divine glory can be kept only in "earthen vessels" (2 Cor 4:7 NABRE). After all, the scandalous and sublime story of the humiliation of the incarnate God cannot truthfully be told in "lofty oratorical, tragic, or epic style." The early Christians made a choice, rejecting the Augustan aesthetic for what can now be called the Augustinian aesthetic. And they did so, Auerbach sees, because they discerned that their art needed to mimic the reality of the incarnation—the atoning of the lowly and the sublime.[23]

Arguably, what Augustine and others realized about Christ's story is true also for all stories, at least if they are meant to bear witness to the truths of the human experience. And insofar as that is true, it holds for pop art as well as high art—for obvious reasons. In "Eulogy," the standout episode in the second season of her Peabody-winning show, *Better Things*, Pam Adlon teaches an acting class. While two students are acting out an ugly breakup scene, Adlon jumps in to offer a critique: "Hold on. You're getting there too easily . . . Where is all this confidence coming from? It's poison for this scene. Throw it away." Later, after another couple plays the same scene, Adlon presses them for being too smooth, too quick.

> The problem is that you're great performers . . . No character you're ever going to play is going to sound like that. You're playing a *person* in this scene. People are weak. They're

not cool and fast. What are your assets as an actor? Your *weaknesses*. Whatever your fears are, whatever you suck at, that's what you've got to tap. That's what people want to see when you're playing people: they want to see you at your weakest . . . They want to see you fail.

In the Gospels, Christ *is* a spectacle, to be sure—just not at all in the way Gibson has imagined. He is a spectacle in the sense that he is put on display for ridicule. He is shown at his weakest, afraid and failing. The soldiers mock him, as do the bandits, and the priests and the scribes and the elders. Even those who love him stand back, grieved and utterly at a loss, without any sense whatsoever that they are seeing God in all his glory. More troublingly, the Father who declared his devotion to the Son at his baptism and again at his transfiguration, in this moment remains silent. As William Congdon's 1960 painting, *Crucifix no. 2*, suggests, Jesus is left so alone that it is as if he is all that is left of creation: everything else has gone dark. There is not even a cross. He is himself the cross, stretched out on nothing, and his head has fallen hard against his chest so that his face is hidden from us and he sees only himself. Gibson's Christ, of course, is the center of attention. He looks up as he dies, and we see his face from above, as if we are in heaven. But Congdon's Christ is curved in on himself, seeing his own end as he is seeing to the work the Father has given him to accomplish on our behalf. Consequently, Gibson's Christ can only be watched, but Congdon's Christ, like the Christ of the Gospels, can be seen—and can make us see.[24]

Approaching Darkness, Unapproachable Light

On the cross, the Son descended alone into incomprehensibility. Unlike anyone else, he experienced death, "not as a biological fact, but as the absolute darkness of hell." Rahner suggests that in a sense, the Son became that darkness but without suffering the pains of hell, because his compassion is unimaginably deeper than all sorrows. His love is more incomprehensible even than death. Hell, in other words, suffers him. He wounds death, mortally, by dying.

> The ultimate fact is the great love which prompted him, in the midst of his own darkness, to say to another who was crucified with him, "Today, you shall be with me in paradise!" and to utter with confidence: "Father, into your hands I commend my spirit!" These words do away with hell! In fact, we could say that the only reason Jesus is not in hell is because he brought the incomprehensible, absolute power of his love into hell with him. It is a terrible thing to fall into the hands of the living God. On the cross, Jesus handed himself over to this God in perfect obedience and love—and there was no endless terror. There was only the blessedness of entering into the still greater love of the God of grace.[25]

In the moment, of course, no one knew what was happening to Jesus. Still, they could sense, somehow, that his death was different. This is why the centurion and his soldiers cry out, "Truly, this was the Son of God" (Matt 27:54 NABRE). It follows, then, that artistic representations of Good Friday are faithful just to the extent that they insinuate this "still greater love," the always deeper incomprehensibility of goodness, which embraces and shelters all things.

As the Fathers said, whatever is assumed is healed and whatever is accepted is transformed.

> [Christ] has accepted death. Therefore this must be more than merely a descent into empty meaninglessness. He has accepted the state of being forsaken. Therefore the overpowering sense of loneliness must still contain hidden within itself the promise of God's blessed nearness. He has accepted total failure. Therefore defeat can be a victory. He has accepted abandonment by God. Therefore God is near even when we believe ourselves to have been abandoned by him. He has accepted all things. Therefore all things are redeemed.[26]

Dying and dead, Christ enters the depths of reality, depths that cannot be experienced, much less represented, constituting that reality for our good. Therefore, Good Friday is the Sixth Day, the day in which humanity is at last created and blessed and entrusted with dominion. And Pilate's declaration is true in ways he and those who first heard it could not even begin to imagine: "Behold, the man!" (John 19:5 NABRE). As Bonhoeffer says, God loves not model human beings or an idyllic world but real people and the real world. "What we find repulsive in their opposition to God, what we shrink back from with pain and hostility . . . this is for God the ground of unfathomable love." God is not repulsed by our ugliness, but drawn to it. He saves us not because we are noble, but simply because we are. And he stands with us against our accusers—against our self-accusations.[27] More than anything else, this is what Gibson seems not to have seen and what *The Passion of the Christ* fails to show.

A Moving Picture

On Good Friday God sets an image before our eyes: our own image, which we have been trying not to see.[28] It is not a spectacle so much as a sight, a picture, and like the best pictures, it tells the truth in a way that makes us face it at last. Christ sees and sees to what we cannot. His beauty is hidden by the ugliness done to him. But at the same time, his beauty, and ours, is mysteriously revealed, because we see in him not only that something is wrong with us and all that we have done wrong, but we see also our goodness, our desirability, our belovedness. These are of course given to us, as everything is, including our existence. But they are truly ours. As St. Paul says, what God suffered, he suffered for our glory. He was given up for our sakes and raised up for our sakes so that through him God might give us all things. The bottom line is: God would rather not be God at all than to be God without us. And this is true for all creation and each creature, including Judas, Christ's mirror image, who betrayed himself in betraying Christ and hanged himself only hours before Christ, who is faithful only to the faithless, was hanged for him.

It is also true for our own creations, however untruthful or humble they prove to be. The gospel dignifies even our poorest or falsest tellings of Jesus' story, including, of course, *The Passion of the Christ*. More importantly, it dignifies *us*, even as our living of the gospel proves false or poor. This, then, is what is best about Good Friday: what happens to and in and through Jesus happens apart from us, although it is entirely for our sake. It happens for us and for our good in spite of the fact that we do not understand it and whether or not we can believe it. This is the true "scandalous force" of the crucifixion, and why it is so hard, perhaps even impossible, to be lost in the end. After all, God promised to himself to accomplish our salvation before we were even created (Titus 1:2). And the promise he makes to us is assured by a covenant he has made with himself (Heb 6:13). Hence, Franz Wright reassures us: "Everyone knows what the cross means, or will/ before long."[29] Understanding that is what it means to believe.

7

The End of All Endings

Easter

Resurrection does not mean that my life starts up again. It means that the life I lived is eternally presented and interpreted within the community of God.

Robert Jenson

Remember Jesus Christ, raised from the dead, a descendant of David—that is my gospel.

2 Timothy 2:8

Dance me to the end of love.

Leonard Cohen

The Sense of an Ending

In a 2001 Veritas Forum lecture, delivered at Duke Divinity School, Jeremy Begbie draws deeply on the work of British literary critic Frank Kermode, contending that to be human is to feel the need for a close to history that redeems and fulfills all that has happened in time—including, of course, all that has happened in one's own life and lifetime. This need for sense-making endings expresses itself unmistakably, Begbie argues, in modern literature and music. So, we cannot help but read and listen in anticipation of an ending that "gives the whole story a unity, gathering the strands together, resolving the discord and the dissonance" into a reconciling and elevating consonance.

According to Begbie, this "sense of an ending" shapes our stories and songs into a necessarily three-part shape: beginning in equilibrium, there is a movement through tension into resolution. He describes it as the movement moves from home, away, and at last comes Home again. The capitalization of the second "Home" is critical, indicating that the return is the culmination of a journey and not simply a relapse or recursion to the beginning. In other words, the movement is not strictly circular. In Begbie's phrasing, we leave and return, but when all is said and done everything is not as it was, although everything is all right. We are home again, but now we are more ourselves, and our home is more itself, than when we first left it.[1]

Begbie agrees with Kermode: this aesthetic sensibility emerged from the Christian experience of the world understood in the light of the sweeping biblical narrative, which, he suggests, "tells the story of the world" in three parts. In the beginning, there is equilibrium. Then, tensions break in, which God must overcome. Finally, God, through Jesus, the son of Abraham, indeed overcomes them, reconciling all differences, at last making his home with his creatures in the "new heavens and the new earth." He sees this same threefold pattern in many of the stories nested within the story, as well. As Begbie recounts it, Jesus' parable of the prodigal son tells how "a young man told his father to drop dead," then fled to a "far country," only eventually to return and, against all odds, is gladly welcomed by his father: "home, away, and Home again."

Intriguingly, Kermode's original argument is that this "sense of an ending" resulted from the failed apocalyptic expectations of the first Christians.[2] They wrongly expected the apocalypse to come quickly. When it did not, instead of abandoning their eschatology altogether, they reinvented it: the imminent was reimagined as the immanent; *chronos* was reimagined as *kairos*.

Naive apocalypticism has been modified to produce (under the pressure and relevance of great new systems of knowledge, technological and social change, of human decision

itself) a sense of ends only loosely related to the older pre-
dictive apocalypse, and to its simpler notions of decadence,
empire, transition, heavens on earth.[3]

Kermode finds this reinvented apocalypticism beautiful, if
untrue. Not without reason, he opens his book with a callback to
the closing lines of Peter Porter's "The Historians Call Up Pain":

> We cannot know what John of Leyden felt
> Under the Bishop's tongs—we can only
> Walk in temperate London, our educated city,
> Wishing to cry as freely as they who died
> In the Age of Faith. We have our loneliness
> And our regret with which to build an eschatology.[4]

In Kermode's analysis, this immanentized eschatology is a distinctly Christian invention, and its first great work was the forma-
tion of the canon, which he describes as the conversion of Jewish
Scripture "into another book entirely" through "an extraordinary
act of fictive imagination." "The book is now a whole, starting
from 'in the beginning' and, since Revelation is placed last in
the book, ending at the end, so that the whole vast collection has
unity, makes one sense, conferred precisely by this transformative fiction."[5] Because our imaginations are shaped by this fiction,
Kermode argues that we expect, even need, our stories to move
from a genesis to a revelation, even while we know full well that
our end will be as purposeless as our beginning was. "In the mid-
dest, we look for a fullness of time, for beginning, middle, and
end in concord."[6] We expect, he says, the *tock* of an eschaton for
every *tick* of a history, including the *tick* and *tock* of our own birth
and death. When all is said and done, however, the stories we tell
have a meaningfulness that the lives we live cannot.

Both Kermode's book and Begbie's lecture give voice to the
now popular idea that Christianity offers a "grand narrative" that
makes sense of everything from beginning to end. This comes
clear, for example, in the widely popular writings of N. T. Wright
and Stanley Hauerwas, two of the best-known contemporary

Christian theologians. Wright, in more or less all of his works, insists that the canon is "irreducibly narrative in form," a "massive narrative structure" enclosing an "overall storyline of astonishing power and consistency." For him, "to think Scripturally is to think narratively."[7] And Hauerwas argues along similar lines, contending that our central and defining moral failure is that "our primary story is that we have no story." In his account, it is only a narrative that we can "live into" that provides us with what we need to "acquire a character sufficient to make our history our own." Hence, he argues, the Christian way of life, rightly understood, is nothing other than "full participation in an adequate story"—the story the Scriptures tell.[8]

Obviously, many find this framework useful. But if we are not careful, it will lead us, without our knowing it, to misread the stories the Scriptures actually tell. Strikingly, Begbie makes exactly this mistake in his single-sentence recounting of the parable of the prodigal son, which does not in fact end in reconciliation. The elder son, who never left home, admits at the last that it has for him always been a far country. And in the end, he is estranged from his father, who has neglected him for years, and from his younger brother, who is now too caught up in his own celebration to come out to greet him. Kermode, for his part, notices that Jesus' parables seem to be "divorced from the consolatory gospels in which they are found." But he is not surprised: of course "the concordant tale" should include in itself irony and paradox; and of course we should expect "inexplicable patterns" and "mazes of contradiction" to emerge in the process of any human attempt at making satisfactory sense of all things.[9] What else would we expect from reality?

The Non-sense of an Ending

But are the Gospels in fact consolatory? Do the canonical texts tell a concordant tale? No, not quite. At least not in the sense that Kermode and Begbie imagine. The conclusion of the First Gospel includes a clear admission that in the final meeting with Jesus some of his disciples doubted (Matt 28:17). But for whatever reason, he does not speak to their questions. He simply sends them forth with a word of strange promise and paradoxical assurance: "All authority in heaven and on earth has been given to me. Go therefore and make disciples of all nations . . . And remember, I am with you always, to the end of the age" (Matt 28:18-20). The uninitiated or negligent reader may read this ending as consolatory and concordant. But the initiated and careful reader knows better. In fact, this ending anticipates Jesus' disappearance—and the disciples' literal and metaphorical descent from the mountain. They had hoped that their master would bring about the end of the ages, and that he would reward them richly for their faithfulness once his kingdom was established. Instead, he leaves them with a promise that he will never leave them, and sends them back to their ordinary lives, burdened with responsibility.

The Second Gospel forces this strangeness on us more bluntly than the other Gospels do. Almost certainly, it originally ended—harshly and abruptly—at 16:8: "So they went out and fled from the tomb, for terror and amazement had seized them; and they said nothing to anyone, for they were afraid." But even the longer ending, added by unsettled scribes, and quickly accepted as canonical, proves to be anything but simply consoling or concordant. In Mark's telling, Jesus appears after his resurrection first to Mary Magdalene, who believes him. But when she shares her news with others, as he had told her to do, they are overcome with sorrows and do not take her report seriously (Mark 16:9-11). Later, Jesus appears to two disciples, whom Mark does not name. But they too are met with disbelief when they share the news that Jesus is alive (Mark 16:12-13). Finally, he appears to the Eleven all at once, rebuking them for their faithlessness and stubbornness (Mark 16:14). He sends them out in mission, performing signs and wonders, but the reader, remembering the disciples' repeated failures and misapprehensions, remembering that even Jesus' final word to them began with reproof, cannot help but wonder if the disciples are really up to the task.

The scenes at the end of the Third Gospel are rather less eccentric and portentous. And its last note seems to be an unequivocally happy one: "they worshiped him, and returned to Jerusalem with great joy; and they were continually in the temple blessing God" (Luke 24:52-53). But Acts, Luke's second volume, ends more like the other Gospels do—not neatly or cleanly, but ambiguously and troublingly. Jesus' final pre-ascension promise—"You will be my witnesses in Jerusalem, in all Judea and Samaria, and to the ends of the earth" (Acts 1:8)—has been fulfilled, but not at all as either the disciples or readers of the story would have imagined or hoped. In Paul's last meeting with the local Jewish leaders in Rome, he prophesies their rejection, echoing the words of Isaiah: "Let it be known to you then that this salvation of God has been sent to the Gentiles; they will listen" (Acts 28:28). This happens, the reader notices, in spite of the fact that "some were convinced by what he said, while others refused to believe" (Acts 28:24). In the final lines, the Evangelist observes that for the following two years Paul proclaimed the kingdom of God, "teaching about the Lord Jesus Christ with all boldness and without hindrance" (Acts 28:31).

Luke Timothy Johnson believes that Luke intends this final vision of Paul as apocalyptic prophet to be "entirely satisfactory." Acts has, in Johnson's view, successfully defended "God's fidelity to his people and to his own word." And it now opens out on the vistas of new possibility in the "continuing life of the messianic people . . ."[10] But how can it be satisfying to discover that God's fidelity to his own word cannot bring about the fidelity of God's people to his word—the very word that unilaterally called them into being and summoned them into covenant? In the opening chapter of Luke's Gospel, the priest Zechariah, filled with the Spirit, celebrates that "The Lord God of Israel" has fulfilled his long-awaited promise: "He has raised up a mighty savior for us . . . as he spoke through the mouth of his holy prophets from of old . . ." (Luke 1:68-70). Finally, at long last, God, the God of Israel, "has shown the mercy promised to our ancestors, and has remembered his holy covenant" (Luke 1:72). At the end of Acts, however, this fulfillment turns out to be unrealized. Or, worse, its realization seems to have been an irreversible disappointment.

The Fourth Gospel ends with a triptych of resurrection appearances, all of which are shot through with disquieting and forbidding ambiguity. In the last of these, Jesus appears to seven of the apostles, two of whom remain unnamed. After a miraculous catch of fish, and after Peter, having realized who is speaking to them, leaps from the boat to swim to shore, Jesus calls the seven to share the breakfast he has made for them. After they have eaten, he initiates a painful conversation with Peter, which ends with a forceful reaffirmation of the apostle's calling and a heavy prediction: "Very truly, I tell you, when you were younger, you used to fasten your own belt and to go wherever you wished. But when you grow old, you will stretch out your hands, and someone else will fasten a belt around you and take you where you do not wish to go" (John 21:18). Earlier, Mary had turned to Jesus at his word (John 20:16). But Peter turns from him at this word, no doubt confused and troubled, and sees the unnamed Beloved Disciple. Defensively or defiantly, he asks about his future, but Jesus refuses to answer: "If it is my will that he remain until I come, what is that to you? Follow me!" (John 21:22). Once again, the Evangelist interrupts his narrative to offer an explanatory aside: "So the rumor spread in the community that this disciple would not die. Yet Jesus did not say to him that he would not die, but, 'If it is my will that he remain until I come, what is that to you?'" (John 21:23-24).

The Beginning of the Good News

We can see, then, that all of the Gospels end strangely. And we know why: the Evangelists, like the figures in the story, are striving to come to terms with the fact that Jesus has been raised from the dead. The women who flee from the tomb are not the only ones who are afraid. What they have seen—and, even more, what they have not yet seen—is too much not only for them but for everyone. This should press us to think again, and much more carefully, about what we mean when we say that Jesus is risen. Clearly, it was not simply comforting for those who first experienced it. It seems to have resolved nothing for them. If anything, it created endless lines of new tensions. Why, then, do so many of us think of it as a happy ending?

First, we need to accept this hard truth and let it settle in: Jesus' life ends as all lives do—in death. As we confess in the creed, he died and was buried. Rightly understood, then, his resurrection is not an event that happens to him after his demise, as one more occurrence, however unexpected, in the succession of events that make up the story of his life, his existence. As Rahner says, resurrection is definitively *not* a "return to the limits of a life restricted by space and time and the facts of biology." The Easter story is not an account of the unexpected "final phase" of Jesus' historical career. Instead, it is the story of the salvation of Jesus' entire life and ministry, including his death and his being dead.[11] Death was not merely an interruption for him. And his resurrection was not a resuscitation. He did not come back to life. He was not raised from the dead in the sense that Lazarus was (John 11:1-44) or as some believed John the Baptist had been (Mark 6:14). He was raised from the dead in a unique sense: "the first fruits of those who have died" (1 Cor 15:20). Now, the life he leads is not the continuation of his human existence, but its eternal fulfillment—its salvation, its deification.

> This earthly life of Jesus is not after all simply past and gone: it *is*; it is completed and eternally valid; it has itself been accepted by God and acknowledged as real; from the human subjectivity of Jesus, it has been gathered out of the mere flux of earthly time into the Now of eternity, and taken into irrevocable possession the real nature of the heavenly intercession of the risen Christ with the Father.[12]

In other words, the resurrected Jesus does not remember what he once did, and act now in ways that are faithful to those memories.

He has not left his earthly occupation behind, and taken up a new one. Nor is his heavenly occupation the mere prolongation of his earthly one. Rather, his intercession for us is eternal because it is the divine validation of the fullness of his human history, a fullness which necessarily includes his death. What is more, his intercession is the way in which God's reality and our reality have been made and still yet shall be made the same reality. Or, to say the same thing another way, it is his presence to God as the one raised from the dead that makes heaven habitable for us.[13] He is the Father's house in which there are many mansions. He does not dwell "out there" in some far-flung corner of the universe. God is God's own space, just as God is God's own time. And the risen Jesus dwells in that space, in that time, making it livable for us and for all things.

This is why confessing that Christ has been raised from the dead is a matter of faith, not conspiratorial knowledge.[14] Believing in the resurrection is categorically unlike believing in aliens. The empty tomb is not a proof, which is why John's Gospel contrasts Peter's and the Beloved Disciple's experiences at the tomb with Mary Magdalene's encounter with the risen Jesus in the garden (John 20:1-18). And this is why in Mark's Gospel the women who have seen the empty tomb and heard the angelic testimony are speechless with fear: they have not yet seen Jesus. As both Paul and the Evangelists make it abundantly clear, Jesus' resurrection appearances were revelations, theophanies. Thus, Jesus showed himself only to those who believed in him, assuring their belief in him precisely by showing himself to them.[15]

This should remind us that the resurrection is an event that happens to time, not merely in it. Strikingly, the Gospels do not describe the event itself. No witness is said to have seen it. The Gospels say only that it has already happened. The stone is rolled away not so that Jesus can leave the tomb, but as a sign that death could not hold him. In Luke, a number of women, including Mary Magdalene, come to the tomb early Sunday morning, "at early dawn," and find the stone rolled away and the tomb empty

(Luke 24:1-2). In John, Mary Magdalene comes alone, "while it is still dark," and sees the stone is removed. Afraid of what that might mean, she rushes back to find Peter and the Beloved Disciple (John 20:1-2). In Mark, Mary Magdalene, Mary the mother of James, and Salome bring spices to anoint Jesus' corpse, "very early on the first day of the week, when the sun had risen," uncertain how they will remove the stone from the face of the tomb. Arriving, they realize with a start that it has already been removed. In the tomb, they find "a young man, dressed in a white robe," who tells them that Jesus is risen, and that they must go and tell Peter and the other disciples that he intends to meet them in Galilee (Mark 16:1-7). In Matthew, Mary Magdalene and "the other Mary" come to "see the tomb" "as the first day of the week [is] dawning." As they stand there, an earthquake tears the earth, and an angel, like a flash of lightning, appears before them, pushing the stone aside and sitting on it. The guards faint, but the angel assures the women that Jesus has already been raised and that they should go quickly and share the news with the disciples, and then together meet Jesus in Galilee. The women rush from the tomb, both afraid and overjoyed, and Jesus, suddenly and unpredictably, appears to them. They fall at his feet, but he again assures them that they do not need to be afraid and encourages them to tell his "brothers" to meet him in Galilee (Matt 28:1-10).

These stories, as well as the icons, songs, liturgies, poems, and films that flow from and point back to them, do not attempt to show either Jesus' death or his resurrection in themselves. They show his dying and his being dead. They show him alive. They show the impact of what happens to others because of his living and dying. This reminds us, then, that death and life are hard limits for us, philosophically and artistically, as well as existentially and historically.[16] We know silence and we know sound. We know darkness and we know light. But we do not know, and cannot know, how it is that light is light and not darkness and how it is that sound is sound and not silence. Therefore, if Jesus is who we believe he is, the events of Easter happen not within our limits but without them, making them what they are, giving them their integrity and purpose. Again, resurrection is eschatological, not merely historical. It is not one more thing that happens to Jesus, but the happening of Jesus to all things. He is not changed: everything is changed. We see, at last, that Christ was risen from the foundation of the world.

We talk sometimes as if the resurrection were merely unusual. But in truth, it is entirely, essentially unlike anything that has happened or ever could happen. It is identical with Jesus himself—a divine, divinized, and divinizing event. Precisely for this reason, we must avoid thinking of it as literal/physical or metaphorical/ spiritual. Updike's "Seven Stanzas at Easter" is glorious, but because it works with this polarity, it is only half right (theologically, at least, if not also artistically). Christ is risen "as his body." But his cells did not rehabilitate and his amino acids did not rekindle. As Scripture insists, what is "sown" in death is "a physical body"—perishable, dishonorable, weak. What is raised is "a spiritual body," in absolute power and imperishability, not merely alive but life-giving (1 Cor 15:42-44). To be sure, Updike is right to warn us against mocking God with metaphor: there is no sidestepping this event; it will not be made into a parable.[17] But resurrection is better understood not as a biological fact but as the creative truth, not as the transformation of a corpse but as the divine establishment of an entire life—and all that was done in that life—as the source, guide, and goal of everything that exists.

Christians confess that Jesus is the Word made flesh, God the Son, born of a woman, living a truly human life. But this "becoming" did not mark a change in God, or make a new set of experiences for him. Assuming human nature, Jesus was not changed but changed it. He was not unwillingly at the mercy of his body, as we are at the mercy of ours. Instead, his body, perfectly aligned with his soul, yielded at every point to his desire. He suffered. But he did not suffer the fact that he was flesh and blood. As Maximus says,

> When he became a human being, he was not subjected
> to nature. On the contrary, he rather raised up nature

to himself and made it another mystery. And while he himself remained completely incomprehensible, and demonstrated his own Incarnation . . . to be more incomprehensible than any mystery, the more he has become comprehensible because of it, the more he is known to be incomprehensible through it. "For he is hidden even after his revelation," the teacher says, "or, to speak more divinely, even in his revelation."[18]

Before his resurrection, Christ's body is divine, divinized, and divinizing—and, just so, authentically human. Maximus agrees with Cyril: "It is *this* flesh, to which properly belong touch, voice, and the rest, that has the power to give life."[19] Thus, what happens in his resurrection is the full and overflowing realization of his already "engodded" humanity. Easter witnesses that realization, the once-for-all breaking forth of and taking in of all things in Christ's risen body, which is his fullness, the fullness which fills all things (Eph 1:23). He did, and does, as John's Gospel says, "tabernacle" among us (John 1:14). But the light of Easter reveals that he does so as the cosmic temple in whom all things exist.

The Gospels insist in no uncertain terms that the body Jesus presents to his disciples is *his* body, the very same one they had touched and heard and seen and smelled. The very same one which underwent crucifixion. It still has marks of torture on it. What Jesus says to Thomas in one place at one time he says to all of the disciples in another: "Look at my hands and my feet; see that it is I myself. Touch me and see; for a ghost does not have flesh and bones as you see that I have" (Luke 24:39). But this does not mean his corpse had been reanimated. It is the same body, but it is not in the same condition. He has "flesh and bones," but he has them in an uncreated manner. His humanity is divinely mysterious—mysterious with the same mystery the Father is, and has, and gives. Therefore, space and time are not limits for him. As Maximus explains, the Word's embodiment is effected and effective everywhere and always in everything. Jesus is now, no less than then, bodily present in time and space. And even then,

as well as now, time and space are what they are at all to him and
to others only because of what they are through him and in him
for others.

For this reason, the end of R. S. Thomas' "Suddenly" comes
nearer the truth than Updike's "Seven Stanzas" does:

> I looked
> at him, not with the eye
> only, but with the whole
> of my being, overflowing with
> him as a chalice would
> with the sea. Yet was he
> no more there than before,
> his area occupied
> by the unhaloed presences.
> You could put your hand
> in him without consciousness
> of his wounds. The gamblers
> at the foot of the unnoticed
> cross went on with
> their dicing; yet the invisible
> garment for which they played
> was no longer at stake, but worn
> by him in this risen existence.[20]

Franz Wright's "Raising of Lazarus," adapted and translated
from a fragment in Rilke's notebooks, comes closer still, perhaps
because it speaks of Jesus as the one acting, not the one acted
upon. Standing at the mouth of the tomb,

> He heard the voice as if from far away,
> beginning to fill with that gesture
> which rose through him: no hand that heavy
> had ever reached this height, shining
> an instant in air.

Jesus hesitates, afraid "*all* the dead might return" at the drop of
his hand. And suddenly Lazarus appears, alone:

pale as though bled,
stooping at the entrance
and squinting at the light,
picking at his face, loose
strips of rotting shroud.

Lazarus' death begins to undo itself. He feels the threat of the undoing, the reversal, and he fears that it might take his life all over again:

All that he could think of
was a dark place to lie down,
and hide that wasted body.
And tears rolled up his cheek
and back into his eyes,
and then his eyes began
rolling back into his head . . .

Now, Lazarus is not the only one who is afraid:

Peter looked across at Jesus
with an expression that seemed to say
You did it, or *What have you done?*
And everyone saw
how their vague and inaccurate
life made room for his once more.[21]

The last lines of Wright's poem, like the last lines of Mark's Gospel, force on us something of a graced, if not graceful, confusion. Those who witnessed this impossibility have had their lives cast into relief by it. Coming to terms with this unexpected truth, they see, suddenly, that their life—notice, their gathered *life*, not their scattered *lives*—is "vague and inaccurate" by comparison. And as it was with them, so it is with anyone who encounters Jesus, who is in himself resurrection life. Peter's expression says it all: we are caught, as he was, right between praise and panic. Just so, we are left neither hopeless nor hopeful. We are left, instead, not unhopeful. We are left afraid, to be sure, but expectantly so: sure that he has done it; not yet sure what he has done.

Knowing the End from the Ending

The anxiety of Easter, like the anxiety of Good Friday, is natural, not demonic. Like Jesus in the garden and on the cross, and like the disciples at his tomb and in their locked rooms, we are afraid not so much because we disbelieve, but because we are not sure, and cannot be sure, what will come of our believing. We trust implicitly in God's almighty goodness. Still, we know that our call to cooperate with that goodness takes us out of our depth, beyond our ken. We are not almighty. We are not even good. We are not afraid of him, exactly. But we are afraid of what might happen to us or be required of us for his and others' sake. All that notwithstanding, we remain confident. Not because we know how it all will end—that knowledge is forbidden to us (Matt 24:36; Acts 1:7). We remain confident because we know, but do not know how we know, that however it all ends, everything that exists and everything that ceases to exist remains nonetheless always open to the God who has raised Jesus of Nazareth from the dead. In that sense, and in that sense only, we can say with Julian: "but all will be well, and all will be well, and every kind of thing will be well."[22]

The Spirit assures us: Christ is risen; therefore, our faith is not vain, the dead have not perished, and we are not to be pitied for our failings, sufferings, and miseries. Still, hope is nothing like optimism. We do not expect a last-second miracle to save us or our world from death. We await Christ, who in the last of his paschal appearances will save us and our reality from the dead, so that death is at last forever "swallowed up" by God's life-giving life (1 Cor 15:54). Death will be no more, because in Christ all of creation will be alive with the Spirit—God's own liveliness—to the Father's delight. Knowing this, we hope "against hope" (Rom 4:18). Knowing this, we know the end from the ending. We know the End is at hand at all times, in every beginning, in every middle, in every ending. This allows us to come to terms with our death and the little deaths that come before it and around it.

In his "Endpoint," the titular poem from his last collection, written in the months and weeks before he died, Updike expresses this spirit wonderfully:

> Why go to Sunday school, though surlily,
> and not believe a bit of what was taught?
> The desert shepherds in their scratchy robes
> undoubtedly existed, and Israel's defeats—
> the Temple in its sacredness destroyed
> by Babylon and Rome. Yet Jews kept faith
> and passed the prayers, the crabbed rites,
> from table to table as Christians mocked.
>
> We mocked, but took. The timbrel creed of praise
> gives spirit to the daily; blood tinges lips.
> The tongue reposes in papyrus pleas,
> saying, *Surely*—magnificent, that "surely"—
> *goodness and mercy shall follow me all
> the days of my life*, my life, forever.[23]

In many ways, the end of the Gospels is more like the close of a poem than like the conclusion of a story. Usually, we expect a narrative to draw all the loose ends together in the end. A poem, too, might afford us the sense of "appropriate cessation," signaling and justifying "the absence of further development."[24] But many good poems give us only trouble, or at least foil our expectations and defer closure. We come away from them provoked, unsettled, disoriented—anything but contented. David Mamet suggests that the best films do this, too, pressing in on us "the visceral introduction of new and transformative information in the last seconds of the film."[25]

At least on some readings, this is the kind of work the Gospels do in their endings. The Evangelists leave us just a bit off balance and more or less on edge, unsure what exactly has happened to Jesus or to those who loved him. All to say, the story of Jesus the Evangelists tell does not quite follow the *equilibrium—tension—resolution* pattern Begbie suggested, any more than the stories of the Old Testament do, or the stories Jesus himself told. Begbie is right that these stories are not simply circular, but he misses the fact that they are also essentially open-ended, unfinished. André Neher speaks of this as the "prophetic return." Jonah's story is paradigmatic:

> When he finally reached Nineveh, Jonah was unhappy, even more unhappy than he had been among the lethal waves. He was unhappy to the point of wanting to die. It was because his voyage had turned out to be a tragedy. Before the return, there had been a rupture. Ulysses returned to the point to which he wanted to return and to which he should have returned. Thus, the circle was completed. This circle protected him against any new adventure, while Jonah, on the other hand, went back to the place which he wished to avoid and ought to have avoided. He wished to avoid it. His embarkation for Tarshish was a flight, an Exodus in the night, towards the antipodes, towards nothingness, in order to get away from God! He ought to have avoided it: His return to Nineveh proved to be useless. Come to proclaim the overthrow of Nineveh, Jonah learned what he most feared: Nineveh was saved! A journey for nothing, a missed return. The circle remains open. For Jonah, the return was a Genesis . . .[26]

Jesus lives the prophetic return, and effects its redemption. Not in a way that closes the circle, but in a way that opens on a new Genesis, which lies on the far side of Revelation. This is a truth that should shape all Christian art as it shapes all Christian artists. Not only narrative, drama, film, poetry, and music, but also architecture, sculpture, painting, and dance can and—insofar as they are meant to be liturgical art—should bring to bear the open-endedness Christ's resurrection created and creates.

I felt this long before I had a name for it. When I was only eight or nine years old, my parents took me to the Five Civilized

Tribes Museum in Muskogee. I wandered around the rooms, listening to the floors creak, until Enoch Kelly Haney's *Emptiness Has a Claim on Death* put itself right in front of my face. It took me down, although I had no idea what was happening or why. Now, I think I sensed, entirely wordlessly, that to be human is to be spirit, and that grief, more than anything else, opens us to the infinity in which our lives are lost and found.

All to say, then, the story the gospel tells is not a story told in three parts, although it may be, among other things, a story about a story told in three parts. The prodigal does go home, go away, and come Home again, arriving where he started and knowing the place for the first time. But, as Jesus tells it, his Home is in need of salvation at least as much as the Far Country is. The reconciliation of the younger son to his father is pointless if it does not open out to include the reconciliation of the sons to each other and to their father. This is why we cannot be satisfied with what happens at the end of Acts. Indeed, it is why we cannot be satisfied with any event or any history, including our own, until all things are made right and God is "all in all."

We cannot be satisfied. But we can be *pleased*. As Updike reminds us, goodness and mercy do follow us all the days of our lives, including our last days, whether they come quickly or slowly, and whether they bring only sorrow or also some joy. Home is not God, not yet; but it can still be good, even now. And the Far Country can be, too. The events of Easter did not secure a happy ending for Jesus and his followers. And they do not promise a happy ending for us. Still, we know that the Spirit is Lord over death as well as life and that the Father gives every origin its originality and every end its finality. We know this because we know Jesus, and the story of his death and resurrection. We know he is the first and last word the Father speaks over every beginning and every ending, a word spoken even if we, like the women fleeing the tomb at the end of Mark's Gospel, say nothing to anyone. Easter is good news, after all—especially for those who are afraid.

8

The Creative Gaze

Ascension

"Ye men of Galilee, why stand ye gazing up into heaven?"
Acts 1:11 AKJV

I don't understand what I saw. I don't even know if I saw it,
since my eyes ended up not being separate from what I saw.
Clarice Lispector

God does not want to be everything.
Jacques Pohier

Something Like an Action of Mercy

Flannery O'Connor's "The Artificial Nigger" ends with what
appears to be a conversion.[1] The ludicrous Mr. Head, finally admit-
ting he is lost in the city he claimed to know so well, finally aware
he has disgraced himself, finally sensing the absurdity of his own
self-image, realizes with a shock that his grandson will never forgive him for his betrayal. And in spite of the fact that against all
expectation he and Nelson have found their way back to the trains
on time, he knows home will never truly be home again:

> He felt he knew now what time would be like without sea-
> sons and what heat would be like without light and what
> man would be like without salvation. He didn't care if he

never made the train and if it had not been for what suddenly caught his attention, like a cry out of the gathering
dusk, he might have forgotten there was a station to go to.[2]

What suddenly caught the old man's attention was a bowed-over
plaster figure, one eye chipped white, holding a piece of discolored
watermelon in its black hand. "An artificial nigger," he exclaimed,
and Nelson rushed to his side, repeating the words in the same
daft tone. For a moment, then, they stood there, stupefied, transfixed, "as if they were faced with some great mystery," side by side
in a perfectly matched attitude: "their necks forward at almost
the same angle and their shoulders curved in almost exactly the
same way and their hands trembling identically in their pockets."
For reasons far beyond their understanding, the figure had seized
them, captivated them, and "in their common defeat . . . [they]
could both feel it dissolving their differences like an action of
mercy." The narrator observes that before this moment, Mr. Head
had never known what mercy felt like, "because he had been too
good to deserve any." But in this moment, he did feel it, or something like it, and it urged him to reassure his grandson with words
that proved his wisdom: "They ain't got enough real ones here.
They got to have an artificial one." The boy nodded in agreement,
shivering: "Let's go home before we get ourselves lost again."[3]

No words passed between them on the journey home, but
stepping off the train into the bright moonlight, Mr. Head felt
"the action of mercy touch him again," and the force of the touch
impressed on him its unsurpassable greatness: "there were no
words in the world that could name it."[4]

> He understood that it grew out of agony, which is not denied
> to any man and which is given in strange ways to children.
> He understood it was all a man could carry into death to
> give his Maker and he suddenly burned with shame that he
> had so little of it to take with him. He stood appalled, judg-
> ing himself with the thoroughness of God, while the action
> of mercy covered his pride like a flame and consumed it. He

had never thought himself a great sinner before but he saw now that his true depravity had been hidden from him lest it cause him despair. He realized that he was forgiven for sins from the beginning of time, when he had conceived in his own heart the sin of Adam, until the present, when he had denied poor Nelson. He saw that no sin was too monstrous for him to claim as his own, and since God loved in proportion as He forgave, he felt ready at that instant to enter Paradise.[5]

O'Connor said all of her stories are about "the action of grace on a character who is not very willing to support it."[6] And that must be what is happening in this story, too, at least if the story is at all what she intended it to be. Perhaps, as one critic suggests, in this moment, at the story's end, the seeds of faith are planted, even though we do not see them flower.[7] Or perhaps the seeds of salvation are not yet planted, much less flowering, but the ground is at least plowed open. But it seems to me the end of this story is ambiguous in a way many, even most, of O'Connor's other stories are not. At the end of "Parker's Back," for instance, O. E., kneeling at his own front door, finally speaks his true name, whispering it through the keyhole: "all at once, he felt the light pouring through him, turning his spider web soul into a perfect arabesque of colors, a garden of trees and birds and beasts." Tattooed and beaten, Obadiah Elihue bears the marks of Christ in his body in a double sense. And in the story's final line, we see him, driven out by his wife but reconciled with himself, his soul made to match his body: "leaning against the tree, crying like a baby."[8] Clearly, *this* is a conversion. "Good Country People," by contrast, ends with something that is almost as clearly an *anti*-conversion: Mrs. Freeman's self-righteousness is only redoubled in the end by what she has experienced, as her last words reveal unmistakably: "'Some can't be that simple,' she said, 'I know I never could.'"[9] It seems clear, then, that it is not quite right to call what happens to Mr. Head a conversion, or even the beginning of a conversion. It is not clear, however, what it should be called. Whatever it is, it is profoundly dark, if not finally unintelligible.

In the last paragraph, which immediately follows the description of Mr. Head's "epiphany," the narrator observes that Nelson watches his old grandfather "with a mixture of fatigue and suspicion." Just then, as the train disappears "like a frightened serpent into the woods," Nelson's face lightens, and he mutters in something like relief: "I'm glad I've went once, but I'll never go back again." It is difficult to know what to make of these last words in this final scene. The disappearance of the serpent-train and Nelson's enlightened face suggest transfiguration—too straightforwardly, in fact. And his last words suggest he has reconciled himself, at last, to the old man's prejudices, which are left, after all they have experienced, fundamentally unchanged.[10] Or perhaps they suggest that he is trying to talk himself into the reconciliation. Regardless, when all is said and done, grandson and grandfather have found each other, but they have not found what they needed most to find. Even if "the great gulf fixed" between them has closed, they remain cut off from the others in the city and so from true knowledge of themselves. Indeed, the chasm between them and "nigger heaven" has only widened and deepened. O'Connor said she wanted to explore in this story "the redemptive quality of the Negro's suffering for us all."[11] But at least on one reading, what overwhelms the monstrous Heads in their shared vision is only that the differences between them are nothing compared to their shared difference from and superiority to "the artificial nigger" and all whom he represents. It is as if they say to themselves and to each other, without words, "Things may be bad between us, but at least we are not niggers."[12]

It is true that the final paragraphs frequently reference the "action of mercy." And much of what Mr. Head is said to feel in his moment of transfiguration rings true to O'Connor's theological vision, at least when read without suspicion. But from the opening paragraphs, the narrator has shown herself to be unreliable. Sometimes, she speaks in her own voice. But quite often

she speaks in a voice that only echoes Mr. Head's thoughts.[13] At
the very beginning of the story, for example, as Mr. Head awakes
to find his room flooded with light, the narrator observes that he
could have told the brooding moon "age was a choice blessing
and that only with years does a man enter into that calm understanding of life that makes him a suitable guide for the young." A
few lines later, she tells us that Mr. Head's "physical reactions, like
his moral ones, were guided by his will and strong character," and
that this moral rectitude "could be seen plainly in his features."
Unquestionably, these are Mr. Head's own thoughts of himself,
simply channeled or mimicked by the narrator, almost certainly
in mockery. But the description which follows is clearly the narrator's truth, which exposes the absurdity of Mr. Head's self-talk:
"He had a long tube-like face with a long rounded open jaw and
a long depressed nose." O'Connor is too accomplished an artist,
and the effect of this device too powerful, for it to have been acci-
dental or mistaken. She, the author, means to leave the reader
feeling the same exhaustion and suspicion the narrator says Nelson feels at the end. But the reader, I suspect, is meant to feel this
not only toward Mr. Head and his poor grandson, but also toward
the narrator, the author—and, most importantly, toward herself.

Tellingly, in the story's decisive scene, the reader is told first
that *both* of the Heads feel something and that what they feel
is mercy-*like*. And given that the following references to mercy
speak only of Mr. Head's experience, and without exception cast
him in a flattering light, much as he imagined the moon at the
beginning dignifying his room, it seems likely, if not quite certain, that Mr. Head is not converted by his encounter with the
Black icon. As critics have suggested, in O'Connor's alchemy,
Black is often white, and darkness often light; and that certainly
seems to be true in this case. The dark face of "the artificial nigger" radiates reality, but the Heads are "enlightened" not by that
reality but by an awareness of their whiteness so sudden and so
powerful they can only imagine it as an act of God. Mr. Head,
then, does experience something like a conversion. But in a

wicked trick, his experience only inverts and elevates his twisted self-image. At the beginning of the story, he is in his own mind a morally upright sage. At the end, he thinks himself a sinner—but an equally great one: "no sin was too monstrous for him to claim as his own . . ." The narrator says Head's pride is consumed in a flame of forgiveness, and yet he is left absolutely sure of his readiness to face God, certain that he has already judged himself with God's own thoroughness.

The Divine-Human Comedy

In many ways, "The Artificial Nigger" reads like an absurdist retelling of Dante's *Divine Comedy*. O'Connor forces that awareness on the reader right from the beginning, in a passage that once again underscores the narrator's devious ways:

> [Mr. Head's] eyes were alert but quiet, and in the miraculous moonlight they had a look of composure and of ancient wisdom as if they belonged to one of the great guides of men. He might have been Vergil summoned in the middle of the night to go to Dante, or better, Raphael, awakened by a blast of God's light to fly to the side of Tobias.[14]

In O'Connor's irreverent revisioning, Mr. Head is his own Virgil, his own Raphael. But he cannot even tell heaven from hell (that is, from "nigger heaven"). And so, neither can his ward, Nelson. The narrator never says if "the city," Atlanta, is up or down from Head's home. But the old man regards it strictly as the abyss, although Dante describes two cities: Dis and Paradise, one below and another above. The poet's journey into the inferno begins in a "shadowed forest" at sunrise, and Mr. Head's anti-journey also begins in a wood, and also at sunrise: "A coarse-looking orange-colored sun coming up behind the east range of mountains was making the sky a dull red behind them . . ." But once Mr. Head and Nelson board the train, it becomes impossible to keep separate the paradisal and the infernal aspects of their experiences, which suggests either that they are in purgatory or that they are so upside down and inside out that they continually mistake one for the other.

At the end of the story, Head and Nelson slog their way out to the city's edges, escaping at last the imagined abyss at its center, and they find themselves in a dreamy, or nightmarish suburbia. They see mansions with perfectly manicured lawns, entirely deserted. There are no sidewalks, only driveways, and these "wound around and around in endless ridiculous circles"—much like the circles of Dante's underworld. They know they have returned to the "white" part of town because they see "big white houses . . . like partially submerged icebergs in the distance," a detail which unmistakably recalls the lake of ice in Dante's lowest round of hell. The old man, at last, has "lost all hope," and the young man's mind is "frozen around his grandfather's treachery."[15] Earlier, near the center of the story, and in the depths of the perceived abyss, Nelson stumbles upon a large Black woman in a tight pink dress, and is utterly overwhelmed by her presence. Her effect on him is plainly erotic, but not merely that; he is moved to adoration: "[he] would have collapsed at her feet if Mr. Head had not pulled him roughly away."[16] This nameless woman is a re-figuration of Dante's Beatrice, or a re-figuration of both Beatrice and Francesca, whom Dante encounters in the second ring of the inferno.[17] But old Mr. Head, the absurd anti-Virgil, mistakes her for a Medusa, and snatches Nelson back. For a moment, the boy is drawn out of himself toward manhood by his desire for the woman, just as Dante was drawn out of himself by Francesca and Beatrice. But Mr. Head's rebuke shames the young man, and reduces him again to childishness: "The sneering ghost he had seen in the train window and all the foreboding feelings he had on the way returned to him and he remembered that his ticket from the scale had said to beware of dark women and that his grandfather's had said he was upright and brave. He took hold of the old man's hand, a sign of dependence that he seldom showed."[18] Mr. Head is anything but a faithful guide. He not only cannot discern hell from heaven, but also he cannot discern what saves from what damns.

At the end of his journey, Dante is led into the empyrean and there sees God, and in God, Christ:

> In the profound and clear ground of the lofty light appeared to me three circles of three colours and of the same extent, and the one seemed reflected by the other as rainbow by rainbow, and the third seemed fire breathed forth equally from one and the other . . . That circling which, thus begotten, appeared in Thee as reflected light, when my eyes dwelt on it for a time, seemed to me, within it and in its own colour, painted with our likeness, for which my sight was wholly given to it. (*Paradiso* 33)[19]

And at the end of his anti-journey, Mr. Head, an imagined angel in the company of imagined devils, also stumbles head-on into something like a beatific vision. He too sees an image "painted with our likeness," a figure "about Nelson's size [and] pitched forward at an unsteady angle," differently colored, like Dante's circles, and sitting on a low brick fence, curved around a lawn. But unlike Dante, Mr. Head does not recognize either God or himself in the image. Instead, he sees only a figure of an entirely inferior, wholly alien otherness. He is taken by the sight of it, of course; but only "*as if* faced with some great mystery" (emphasis added). And so he is spurred to talk at precisely the moment Dante found himself reduced to silence: "He looked at Nelson and understood that he must say something to the child to show that he was still wise and in the look the boy returned he saw a hungry need for that assurance. Nelson's eyes seemed to implore him to explain once and for all the mystery of existence." And what Mr. Head says exposes what he in fact believes is the mystery of existence: blacks should know their place, and whites should be grateful for theirs.

Because the narrator is so perfectly unreliable, it is easy to misread this story. One critic, for example, gets it exactly wrong. He recognizes it as a grotesque retelling of *The Divine Comedy*, and celebrates it as not only O'Connor's best work but also "one of the best allegories in American literature since Hawthorne." But he misreads the vision scene entirely:

> The statue is a revelation. It is inscrutable and mysterious, a symbol of universal suffering. Standing before it, Nelson and Head are literally transformed. "Mr. Head looked like an ancient child and Nelson like a miniature old man." Head's name has been ironical throughout the story, for reason has not proven sufficient to save the soul; this depends on grace, which Nelson and Head perceive through the statue of the artificial Negro. Both of them are forced to confess to the ultimate mystery of things. Both do penance, and are purified. The earlier allusion to Raphael coming to Tobias is now clear—the grandfather and grandson have been taught to rely on God's aid, and His power . . . Head and Nelson acquire grace. As pilgrims they recognize their sins, public and private. The image which they leave is a geography, a journey of the soul, reminding us that we go to heaven by walking on real roads.[20]

The image *is* a revelation, but not because it is either inscrutable or mysterious, and, above all, not because it symbolizes universal suffering. If it symbolizes suffering, it is a very particular, entirely scrutable and unmysterious suffering: the suffering of Black families and Black persons. But it is perhaps nearer the truth to say that the figure epitomizes white power, at least as the Heads see it. After all, this statue sits on a fence in a white suburbia as a kind of trophy, a token, or, better, a totem of white superiority, asserting the right of those in power to make and use and be amused by whatever they make of the Black person. And this totem-trophy engenders in these two anti-pilgrims exactly what such things are meant to engender. So, no, the Heads do not see grace in the statue. Blinded, they see only its total gracelessness, and so feel a sudden appreciation for their own dignity, which they feel, not without gratitude, that "nature," that is, God, has given them. They do not recognize their sins, public or private, and they do not "acquire grace," or do

penance, and they are in no sense purified. Their racism is subli-
mated, not eradicated. When all is said and done, because he cannot see the reality of his own image in the face of "the artificial
nigger," Mr. Head's salvation is itself artificial.[21] Dante's vision alters
him, absolutely. The love he sees "revolves," revolutionizes, him. But
Mr. Head's vision merely affects him, and leaves him unturned—a
mock epiphany, a failed revolution.

Beside the Light, and in It

But in truth, at its deepest, this is not a story about artificial grace
and false conversions, although it does lay bare the rot at the
heart of so much that passes for Christianity in the American
South, a Christianity in almost every instance more or less fully
complicit with racist ideals and systems. Instead it is a story about
the power, or powerlessness, of the uncreated image of God in the
figures we create. In one sense, as I have already suggested, the
"artificial nigger" epitomizes white supremacy, and so symbolizes
nothing. But the even deeper truth is that the "artificial nigger"
is more than a symbol: it is, in the exact sense, a *mystery*. And
it is mysterious precisely because it is more and other than the
makers intended it to be. Indeed, it irrefutably contradicts the
message they hoped to send. They sought in this work to profane
and vulgarize the image of God, to reduce it to triviality and so
to efface its grace. But in fact, their work discloses a secret: only
what is holy can be profaned, and no profanation can obscure
that sanctity entirely. Whatever we create, however hateful, witnesses in spite of itself to the grace of creation. Hence, the artificiality of the image, as well as the artificiality of the name ("nigger")
given to it, cannot fail to lift up the inexorable givenness of the
very reality it wants so badly to wipe away.

The Divine Comedy is said to be "the summa in verse." And
O'Connor's retelling is no less indebted to Aquinas' theology. But
her dark and inglorious Christ figure is perhaps even truer to that
theology, or at least more movingly so, than Dante's brilliant and
glorious one. The poet's vision of God sanctifies him. Mr. Head's

vision merely affords him the heady feeling of having been sanctified. But precisely in its powerlessness, its seeming inefficacy, O'Connor's Christ as "artificial nigger" shows something new, something unforeseen, in the depths to which Christ descends in identifying with us, not only sharing our nature, which is fashioned in his image, but sharing the nature of the things we have fashioned to denature ourselves or others. Ultimately, "the artificial nigger" is ridiculous because white supremacy is ridiculous, and Mr. Head is ridiculous because he embodies it. But O'Connor's Christ assumes that ridiculousness as his own, tying himself to the oppressors by taking on not only their likeness but even the oppressive likenesses they make of those they oppress.

Seeing God, Dante finds he cannot turn away: "At that light one becomes such that it is impossible for him ever to consent that he should turn from it to another sight; for the good which is the object of the will is all gathered in it, and apart from it that is defective which there is perfect" (*Paradiso* 33).[22] But the Heads do look away, look to each other, all too easily. And this exposes their untruthfulness, of course. But it also reveals Christ's truthfulness: he does not absorb attention, but deflects it, redirecting it up toward the Father, out toward the neighbor, down and in toward the self. As Aquinas says, the incarnation is fitting precisely because "it belongs to the essence of goodness to communicate itself to others . . ." (*ST* III.1.2). That is, the divine life is essentially a giving and a receiving, a going out, a moving away from, as well as a coming back in, a returning to—even if it is a returning through what has been broken or left in ruins. Therefore, Christ, in his incarnation, bodies forth that reality. This is the mystery in his claim, "Whoever has seen me has seen the Father" (John 14:9), and in his challenge to the rich young ruler: "'Why do you call me good?' Jesus answered. 'There is no one good but God alone.'" (Mark 10:18). Jesus images the Father precisely by refusing to be a static object of adoration, and this is why he is not only a body who can be seen and heard and touched, but a way of seeing, hearing, and touching. To look *at* him rightly is to look *along* him at God and neighbor, and to see in and with and through them, everything else.[23] He will not allow us simply to gaze at him. He redirects our gaze so that we see ourselves, and one another, differently, gracefully.

In the incarnation, the Son translates his way of living the divine life into creatureliness, a way which is inherently deferring and preferring. He becomes an object, a thing, a fact. He is and remains the uncreated truth, of course, but as a creature he is available to and present with other creatures, alongside them, as one among them. In the ascension, this way of living the creaturely life is translated back into uncreatedness, into the full and unbroken communion that is the ground and goal of all that exists. This is why Jesus says to Mary in the garden, "Do not hold onto me, for I have not yet ascended to the Father" (John 20:17). And why he says to Thomas, "Blessed are those who have not seen and yet have believed" (John 20:29). This is the mystery celebrated on the feast of ascension: Christ's humanity, living and dead, is made integral to God's way of being God, so that it is the source of all that exists. In the language of Colossians, Jesus is "the firstborn of all creation" just because he is "the firstborn from the dead." After his ascension, he is not available as he had been before, as one more fact or factor among others. And in this sense, Ascension Day is a "festival of holy pain."[24] But now, he, who once was known "after the flesh," is available as the truth of all facts and factors, infusing all that exists, and all that ceases to exist, with the mystery of his own life. Indeed, in his ascension it is revealed that even that "before" and that "after" are determined by what he did in and between them. And so, in this sense, Ascension Day is also a "festival of the future of the world." As Rahner says, "He holds eternally within himself the results of creation's history as his own reality, and lets it participate in his own life for all eternity."[25] Christ is risen from the foundations of the world. And that is why not only creation itself but also our creations, however rich, however poor, always yield more than we intend or can constrain.

Dante's *Divine Comedy* ends with a cascade of redirecting, redirected gazes. At the end of *Paradiso* 32, following Beatrice's words with his eyes, Dante is led toward Mary, the queen of heaven, whom he encounters at the opening of the final canto. And, as Beatrice had advised him, he asks for her intercession—that he might see God, and that he might "keep his affections pure after so great a vision." Then she directs him toward the throne with her gaze, too: "The eyes by God beloved and reverenced . . . were directed to the Eternal Light . . ." And Bernard does the same: "[he] signed to me with a smile to look upward." But Dante finds he is already looking that way, because "my sight, becoming pure, was entering more and more through the beam of the lofty light which in itself is true." Charles Williams suggests that in his vision, "Dante is the Knower, and God is the Known, and Beatrice is the Knowing."[26] But another reading of the last lines of the *Paradiso* suggests otherwise, because in spite of the fact that Dante claims it is impossible to look away from seeing God, he in fact does look away. If he had not, he would never have written his poem. And while it seems, in the end, that he forgets Beatrice (and himself and Mary and Bernard), in truth it is the one whom he sees beyond the world that illuminates his seeing of those who are in the world. He is moved to love others as Beatrice was moved, at the beginning of the journey, to love him. Against his own expectations, then, he finds he can "look away" because God is no less present in what is not God than God is in himself. "O Light Eternal, that alone abidest in Thyself, alone knowest Thyself and, known to Thyself and knowing, lovest and smilest on Thyself!" (*Paradiso* 33).[27] In these subtle lines, Dante reveals God's own redirecting gaze, which enlightens Mary's eyes, and God's own signifying smile, which lights up Bernard's face. And in the final line, the poet reminds us that the light of God is a light that *moves*, and moves not only the sun and the other stars, but everyone and everything else with them, so we always dwell in the light and are never not illumined by it.[28] In spite of what Williams suggests, then, God desires not simply to be known, but to be the knower and in all knowers, and to be the knowing and in all knowing, which is why the vision of God ends in a glorious revisioning of all things.

In John's Gospel, the first of Christ's signs is the converting of water to wine: "Jesus did this . . . and revealed his glory; and his disciples believed in him" (John 2:11). And yet, it seems clear that the steward, the bride and the bridegroom, and their guests, do not know what Jesus had done. Even the disciples do not know. No one knows, except the servants who carried the water, and, perhaps, his mother, who provoked him to act in the first place. And the same thing happens at the end of the Gospel, when Peter and "the other disciple" see the empty tomb and believe, even though they do not understand what they have seen (John 20:8-9). There is no ascension in John's Gospel, just as there is no transfiguration and no Last Supper, and all for the same reason: to help us see that because Christ has ascended, all things may be transfigured as they are being offered up in love. This is why he says it is "expedient" for him to "go away":

> Nevertheless I tell you the truth: it is to your advantage that I go away, for if I do not go away, the Advocate will not come to you; but if I go, I will send him to you . . . When the Spirit of truth comes, he will guide you into all the truth; for he will not speak on his own, but will speak whatever he hears, and he will declare to you the things that are to come. He will glorify me, because he will take what is mine and declare it to you. (John 16:7, 13-14)

The Spirit of truth is true just in that the Spirit's relation to the Son, like the Son's to the Father, is reflexive. Neither the Father, nor the Son, nor the Spirit is self-referential. The Spirit refers to the Son, who in turn refers to the Father, who in turn refers to the Son, who in turn refers to the Spirit. This is why the ascension was necessary, and why, as St. Thomas says, it is the cause of our salvation (*ST* III.57.6). In these turnings, and only in these turnings, the one God is made known as modest, humble, deferential, unassuming. To understand this is to understand our own nature, and to be freed to live it. Seeing that God is glorified not in being seen but in seeing to the joy of others, we receive sight. And in the light of his modest glory, we see how to live the same eucharistic, transfigured, and transfiguring life Christ lived and lives.

Christ (and) the Stranger

In a poem dedicated to the Pantocrator mosaic in the medieval Byzantine monastery in Daphni, Greece, Rowan Williams meditates on its odd, unsettling features. Typical Pantocrator icons portray Christ as serene and assured, looking directly at the worshipper, the Gospels held in one hand, the other hand lifted up in blessing. But the Daphni Pantocrator breaks all of these conventions: "Christ's eyes look not at the worshipper but away to one side, and the perspective of the eyes is strangely distorted. Instead of holding a book with serene authority, the figure clutches it with long, desperate fingers. The right hand is lowered; it imparts no teaching, communicates no blessing."

> Pillars of dusty air beneath the dome
> of golden leaden sky strain to bear up
> his sweaty heaviness, his bulging eyes
> drawn inwards to their private pain,
> his hand arthritic with those inner knots,
> his blessings set aside.
> He has forgotten us, this once,
> and sees a black unvisitable place
> where from all ages to all ages he will die
> and cry, creating in his blood
> congealing galaxies of heat and weight.
> Why should he bless or need an open book?
> We know the words as well as he,
> the names, Alpha, Omega,
> fire from fire, we know your cry
> out of the dusty golden whirlwind, how you forget
> us so that we can be.[29]

For Williams, this is an icon of Holy Saturday. Instead of the familiar face of our friend, our brother, we see only the disfigured face of a stranger immersed in an experience that seems to bracket us out. "His thoughts are sealed up in a place beyond our reach . . . In a moment of forgetfulness, he glances into that 'black unvisitable place,' the abyssal horror of Gethsemane and Golgotha."[30] But perhaps it is (also) an Ascension Day icon, an icon of Holy Thursday. Seen this way, the Christ figure is not a stranger, but one who loves others beside us, others strange to us but not to him. He looks past us, not because he has "forgotten us," but because he remembers them, and he is redirecting our gaze to those we have forgotten. He is agonized, even angry, not with us but for them, and his expression pressures us to turn away from him toward them, to visit them in their unvisitable places. And in that turning, that revolution, we become his unfamiliar face, his teaching, his blessing. We are not looking at the light, only; we are also looking along it, at all things enlightened by it. This is what it means to be converted.

Mr. Head was not converted, not truly. And yet, his encounter with the Black Christ cannot be shaken off so easily. As Rahner says, the best stories are stories in which a character "achieves a radical self-confrontation, in which he realizes what he himself is." Of course, as happens with Mr. Head, self-confrontation may lead not toward God but away from him, toward "guilt, perversity, self-hatred, and even demonic pride." Still, to have met Christ in the face of another is to have been left in a "blessed peril."[31] And even if we turn from him, we cannot escape the one who keeps turning, who circles into our lives again and again and again, until at last our desires are aligned with his so that we turn not against him, but with him toward all those he loves.

9

Fire and Ashes

Pentecost

Without the soul and without the city, we cannot help anyone.

Gillian Rose

We must really get down to it and do what Christianity has never done: Concern ourselves with the damned.

Albert Camus

Let us go forth therefore unto him without the camp, bearing his reproach. For here have we no continuing city, but we seek one to come.

Hebrews 13:13-14 AKJV

The City and the Soul

The spine of Gillian Rose's argument in *Mourning Becomes the Law* is her reading of Nicolas Poussin's *Landscape with the Ashes of Phocion (Collected by His Widow)*. As the title suggests, the painting depicts a scene from Plutarch's life of Phocion, which tells the story of an Athenian general's sudden fall from his city's graces after a lifetime of virtuous civic service. In the end, his unyielding truthfulness costs the statesman everything. He is unjustly found guilty of treason, and executed—forced, like Socrates, to drink hemlock. Afterward, his body is burned outside the city, and his ashes are left untended on the pyre. Having briefly sketched this history, Rose explains what the painting, which she saw on Sister Wendy Beckett's BBC show, "Odyssey," shows: "The painting shows Phocion's wife with a trusted woman companion. They have come to the place outside the city wall where the body of Phocion was burnt so that Phocion's wife may gather his ashes—for if they are left unconsecrated, his unappeased soul will wander forever."[1]

According to Sister Wendy, Phocion's wife gathering the ashes represents an act of perfect love—an act appropriate to "the New Jerusalem," the city of justice—an act which stands in definitive contrast with the tyranny of "Athens," the city of injustice. But Rose rejects Sister Wendy's "new ethics" and her interpretation of Poussin's painting. To set redeeming love against the political order, the soul against the city, as Sister Wendy does, is not only to efface the politics of the painting but also to obscure a fundamental reality of our existence: human beings are by nature political as well as moral animals. Thus, in Rose's vision, we are meant to achieve soulfulness for the city's sake, and the city is meant to exist in service to that achievement. "Without the soul and without the city, we cannot help anyone."[2]

Rose, unlike Sister Wendy, interprets Poussin's painting as a call for political resistance and civic renewal. On her reading, Phocion's widow is redeeming both her husband's memory and her city's hope as she and her companion together stage "a protest against arbitrary power," not in defiance of power or law as such, but in anticipation of a return to justice: "Phocion's condemnation and manner of dying were the result of tyranny temporarily usurping good rule in the city." But that good rule can be reestablished. The usurpation can itself be usurped. "This act is not therefore solely one of infinite love: it is a finite act of political justice."[3]

Rose notes that like Phocion's widow buried her husband, Sophocles' Antigone buries the body of her brother in defiance of the law and the rulers. And she observes that in these "delegitimate acts of tending the dead," acts which are illegal but nonetheless just and justifying, these women "reinvent the political life of the community." Risking their lives "on the right and rites of mourning," they carry out "that intense work of the soul" that comes only in grief. This work is necessary whenever a loved one is lost, because without grief we cannot "allow the other fully to depart, and hence fully to be regained beyond sorrow." But it is all the more necessary whenever a loved one is lost to injustice, as these women's loved ones were. And it is necessary not only for the bereaved but also for the polis and all of its powers—the rules, the ruled, and the rulers. "When completed, mourning returns the soul to the city, renewed and reinvigorated for participation, ready to take on the difficulties and injustices of the existing city." But more than that, mourning also calls the city to return to its own soul: "mourning becomes the law."[4] This, Rose suggests, is the significance of the "magnificent, gleaming, classical buildings," which "frame and focus" Phocion's widow's act of political disobedience. For Rose, the buildings in Poussin's Athenian city "convey no malignant foreboding, but are perfect displays of the architectural orders." They present the solidity and magnificence of "the rational order, which throws into relief the specific act of injustice perpetrated by the current representatives of the city—an act which takes place outside the boundary wall of the built city."[5] The orders of the city witness against the disordered uses of power, and this moves us to mourn but not without hope.

In Rose's judgment, the longing to abandon Athens for the New Jerusalem is born of a "phantasised desire" for a humanity without vulnerabilities and a community freed from all difficulty and every separation—a city without walls.[6] This desire for "unbounded mutuality," she insists, in fact "ruins the possibility of political action."[7] And without political action, we are left only with violence of one kind or another. We may more or less succeed in unmaking Athens, but we cannot in fact establish the New Jerusalem. Instead, we will have made for ourselves a new Auschwitz. To that end, what is needed, then, Rose contends, is a truly worldly ethics, a commitment to the common good that is neither naive nor perfectionistic. We must come to terms with the fact that rationality, law, and politics are neither inherently just (as the moderns presumed) nor inherently unjust (as postmoderns fear). We must protest not knowledge and power as such, but their arbitrary and abusive uses. And we must face up to the unavoidable risks of community life, accepting the call to mourn.

This is why Rose so unequivocally rejects what she calls the "Buddhist Judaism" of Emmanuel Levinas, calling instead for a return to rabbinic/prophetic Judaism, which, in her judgment, rightly refuses to be "sublimely passive," staking itself on the certainty of two beliefs: "transcendent justice" does not destroy but establishes the political, and the moral life leads not to the negation of the self but to its maturation and flourishing. Levinas, at least on her reading, wants to prefer the other so radically that otherness itself is once and for all overcome. "To become ethical, this self is to be devastated, traumatized, unthroned, by the commandment to substitute the other for itself."[8] Levinas wants, in other words, to establish the New Jerusalem in place of the old Athens, effecting the end of history in order to leave behind all loss, even the risk of loss. Rose, however, argues that we must learn to live in the "broken middle," rejecting all idealisms, including moral idealisms "masquerading as love," accepting the "perennial anxiety" that comes in sharing a common life, never forgetting the risks, working relentlessly toward a "good enough justice."[9] Instead of pining for an imagined Jerusalem, in which all tears have been wiped from our eyes, we should learn to weep outside our Athens, grieved by its failures to be true to its high calling, grieving until our souls are renewed and the city itself is called to the same renewal. We must, therefore, learn to learn, and this is done, Rose explains, "precisely by making mistakes, by taking the risk of action, and then by reflecting on its unintended consequences, and then taking the risk, yet again, of further action, and so on."[10]

The City without Walls

Without question, there is wisdom in Rose's vision, wisdom that Christians, whether Catholic or Protestant, conservative or progressive, should heed.[11] But is it truly *prophetic*? She rightly warns us against romanticizing otherness or shunning political engagement. And she is right to say Phocion's wife's gathering of her disgraced husband's ashes was a "finite act of political justice" and not "solely one of infinite love." But what she misses, or seems to miss, at least in this work, is that finite acts of political justice are possible only because they are acts of infinite love, and that as such they call the powers and their orders into question, requiring them to answer to those in their care and for those who have been abandoned outside the gates.[12]

In the third of his eight visions, the postexilic prophet Zechariah sees a man with a line measuring the length and breadth of Jerusalem. Watching, he overhears one angel order another to share with the surveyor a word of promise: "Jerusalem shall be inhabited like villages without walls, because of the multitude of people and animals in it. For I will be a wall of fire all around it, says the LORD, and I will be the glory within it" (Zech 2:3-4). Like Haggai, his near contemporary, Zechariah anticipates the final fulfillment of God's promises, the eternal establishment of God's rule in the messianic age to come. But unlike Haggai, who expects that end to come about "in a little while" (Hag 2:6), Zechariah realizes that precisely because God's rule is already at hand, social transfiguration is both possible and necessary. His is a "long-term messianism,"[13] perfectly attentive to the defenseless and disadvantaged, and wholly unimpressed with the prosperous and powerful, because it rests in the nearness of God. He sees in the future a city built without walls because God himself dwells within it and it dwells wholly within God. And he sees at its heart a temple built by exiles once "afar off," but are now brought near, for the sake of the nations. That is the vision that illumines for Zechariah both the past and the present of his people, exposing why they had been driven into exile in the first place and revealing what they must do now in the first waves of restoration. And what he saw shows us the true nature of prophetic vision, which is known to be true because it affords us both urgency and patience, boldness and modesty at once; impressing on us the truth that God is concerned first with those we consider last, and requiring us to take full responsibility for what happens to our neighbors, especially those who cannot care for themselves.

In the light of this prophetic vision, Poussin's painting—and Rose's reading of it—look altogether different. The agony in the body of the widow, and the alarm in the body of her companion,[14] terrified that Phocion's widow may suffer the same fate as her husband for this act of necessary but unlawful honor, as well as the exhaustion in the body of the boy hiding in the shadows behind them, lay bare the sickening indifference of the city's magnificent structures, and even nature itself—the trees are in bloom, and skies are strikingly blue—as well as the inhabitants within the city's walls, who go on with their study, their sport, their prayers, or their conversations without a care either for the evil that has happened or for those who continue to suffer because of it. To be sure, Rose is not wrong to say that this gathering of ashes is a political one. And it will, without doubt, provoke renewal, precipitating a return to compassionate rationality and the righteous use of the law. But this is true only because it first rouses God to act against those who "refused to listen, and turned a stubborn shoulder, and stopped their ears in order not to hear" the word of God that runs sometimes with, sometimes against the grain of the law (Zech 7:11-12). Mourning becomes the law only if, only after, those who make the law remember those who have been made to mourn just as God remembers them. As Zechariah saw, the only city which can hope to be called the city of God is one that is made and remade by those and for those once forsaken outside its walls.

The Politics of Jesus and the New Order of the Spirit

The silence of Poussin's painting calls us into the same silence the word of the prophet warns us to shelter in: "Be silent, all people, before the LORD; for he has roused himself from his holy dwelling" (Zech 2:13).[15] Fittingly, then, it is the *noise* of Pentecost—the wind rushing through the upper room, the voices rising in the temple courts—that answers that silence, and reveals the church's political vocation.

Of course, many Christians, including many Pentecostals, regard Pentecost as anything but a political event. As they see it, the Spirit comes now, as he did at the first Pentecost, on those who have hidden themselves away, catching them up one by one in mystical rapture, arresting the attention of outsiders with the electrical fervor of their devotion, impressing on them their desperate need for salvation. Some but not all hold that this reception of the Spirit affords contemporary believers the power to perform "signs and wonders," just as the apostles did, as well as the authority to dictate what happens in "the supernatural realm." So understood, Pentecost is the paradigmatic *religious* event, calling us to lives of all-consuming devotion, miraculous exploits, and extraordinary, ever increasingly life-altering experiences. It is political only in the sense that it sets us apart from everyone else, granting us preternatural powers, and freeing us from the normal course of life and the civic responsibilities it forces on others. For those who hold this view, the fire of Pentecost is the fire of *revival*.

But Luke's account of Jesus' life and death is overtly, unambiguously political. At the end of the Gospel, Jesus enters Jerusalem during the tense Passover season, riding a donkey's colt. The crowds welcome his "triumphal entry" with songs and shouts of revolution, expecting him to lead a revolt. But instead of claiming his right to the throne, he weeps over the city. Then, he enters the temple courts, and drives out the merchants, cursing their work as robbery. In the following days, he condemns the temple's tax system, denounces the temple authorities for their pretensions and abuses, and foretells the temple's imminent destruction. He also calls into question what is owed to Caesar. Within days, he is arrested, condemned, and executed as an insurrectionist.[16] His accusers denounce him to Pilate: "We found this man perverting our nation, forbidding us to pay taxes to the emperor, and saying that he himself is the Messiah, a king" (Luke 23:2). Pilate finds the charges unwarranted, but agrees, under pressure, to have him crucified. And he had a sign nailed to Jesus' cross: "This is the King of the Jews" (Luke 23:38).

Pentecost, then, for Luke, validates Jesus' sovereignty and declares the continuation of his mission. As Peter makes clear in his address to the bewildered crowd, the resurrected Christ, enthroned with God, has declared war against God's enemies. And in pouring out the Spirit upon his disciples, he has authorized them as his envoys in this end-of-the-age conflict. This is why Peter cites Joel's prophecy, which proclaims "a new world order energized by the movement of the Holy Spirit," one which defies and promises to destroy the worldly orders that "find slavery useful."[17] The coming of the Spirit empowers slaves and women and children—as well as men, young and old—to speak with God's authority. And this foretells the necessary undoing of the old world, built—in God's name, but not with God's blessing—on the subjugation of slaves and women and children. God is the God who shakes the foundations. And the coming of the Spirit's new order, inaugurated at Pentecost, uncovers the corruption of the status quo, and assures the undoing of all social and political arrangements, whether spoken or unspoken.

Drawing on Hannah Arendt's account of power as the opposite of violence, Daniela Augustine argues that the church is a community constituted and inspired by the Spirit to work together toward a full and fully shared flourishing. Because we have already been welcomed into God's hospitality, Christians find ourselves freed to live together in an "unceasing movement of covenantal love," seeking to bring about the all-inclusive and across-the-board justice and peace that God desires for everyone and everything.[18] Not that we are always faithful to this form of life, obviously. But when and where we are, in that moment we humanize one another and so body forth Christ's wisdom, even if only partially and fleetingly. Perhaps we cannot say, as Augustine does, that the church is the *cure* for violence. But without question, as Christ's friends, we can and must curse it—especially when it is deployed in his name—and care for those who have been harmed by it, even if we cannot heal them.

God is not violent. Indeed, because God is love, and because his nature and character are identical, God cannot be violent. What he does is always only the good that holds us in being and invites us toward wholeness. Still, because of what evil and the fear of death have done to us, individually and collectively, and because of our complicity with injustice, we often experience grace as a violation. And it is true that the fire of the Spirit is the fire of the divine wrath. As Jesus says, nearing his fate in Jerusalem, "I came to bring fire to the earth, and how I wish it were already kindled! I have a baptism with which to be baptized, and what stress I am under until it is completed! Do you think I have come to bring peace to the earth? No, I tell you, but rather division!" (Luke 12:49-50). In the garden of Gethsemane, he first tastes this fire. And on the cross, outside the city, he is submerged in it—not as the Father's victim, but as his agent. He does not suffer the Father's rejection; instead, precisely as the Father's beloved, he suffers evil for our sake. And in this suffering, he enters into our estrangement, making it his own in order to unmake it for our sakes. He who is our peace accepts our troubledness, our dis-ease, and divides it from us so we can be reconciled to one another and so to God.

Catching Fire

Poussin's *Adoration of the Golden Calf* depicts the moment Moses descends from Sinai to find the Israelites worshipping before the calf Aaron has made for them. The stately calf dominates the center of the painting, spectacularly pedestaled above the people who are shown crowded around it. Some are dancing, laughing, and bathed in light. Others are praying, ecstatic, and mostly in shadow. A few stand at a distance, wary, and a couple of women are frightened to see that Moses has returned, bearing the tables of the Law. But all of them are oblivious to the black clouds gathering ominously above them. At the edge of the camp, Moses in a fit of rage smashes the tables to pieces against the rocks. Joshua reels in shock. And in the heart of the rising clouds, a golden fire burns. For Christians, this fire is the fire Christ brings to the earth, the divine wrath he both personifies and undergoes. On the day of Pentecost, this is the fire that falls.

For many, as I have said, the fire of Pentecost is the fire of revival, the fire of enthusiasm. But no one has seen more clearly than James Baldwin did that this enthusiasm far more often than not effectively stymies the true work of the Spirit. As he said of his experience in the Black Pentecostal churches of his youth, "The transfiguring power of the Holy Ghost ended when the service ended, and salvation stopped at the church door."[19] He discerned that revivalist enthusiasm fails because it is almost invariably energized by torturous fictions about the wrath of God—either fearing it will fall on us for our wrongdoings or wishing it to fall on our enemies for theirs. But these fictions always only lead to ever-escalating self-condemnation and hatred of others. And inevitably, we build "ladders to fire," condemning all we hate to the flames in hopes of eradicating our own fear, which fuels that hate.[20] But our wrath, unlike God's, increases evil rather than consuming it.

God's wrath comes first against the satanic powers within the city—the political, religious, and cultural elites masquerading as ministers of law and light. It is true, as the writer of Hebrews makes clear, that Christ "suffered outside the city gate" (Heb 13:12). But before he is killed without the city, he is condemned within it. Like Legion, like the criminals who are crucified with him, Jesus is put out of the city because he is recognized as a threat to its establishments. The controlling powers want not merely to kill him, but to expose him to shame as an outcast. So, before he gives himself over to death outside the city in solidarity with the outsiders, he lets himself be handed over to the principalities in order to expose the injustice and folly of their judgments. He is misjudged as an innocent among the innocent before he dies as a pariah among pariahs. The powers do this to him, as they do it to others, in order to make a spectacle of him, a warning sign. But he turns their spectacle against them, reducing their wisdom to nothing by his foolishness, triumphing over them in his defeat, disarming them in his torments (Col 2:15). This is why St. Paul says they would not have crucified him if they had known what they were doing (1 Cor 2:8).

Having condemned the condemnation imposed on him by the satanic powers within the city, Jesus brings God's wrath to bear against the demonic powers at work outside of it—the powers of lawlessness, devastation, and shame. For the sake of our consecration, he died not in the sacred place but in the place of desecration, enduring the fate reserved for the carcasses of animals whose blood was sacrificed. "For the bodies of those animals whose blood is brought into the sanctuary by the high priest as a sacrifice for sin are burned outside the camp" (Heb 13:11). We, in turn, are called to "go to him outside the camp and bear the abuse he endured" (Heb 13:13), sustained by our confidence in him as the one who builds the city that is to come, a truly lasting city (Heb 13:14). And it is precisely that confidence that frees us to live in the city as it is now, knowing it cannot last. Without falling either into despair or naivete, we can live sacrificially, as he did and does, dedicating ourselves to prayer, doing good and sharing all we have, entrusting ourselves to those who are called to care for us (Heb 13:15-19). He has made an example of the rulers and authorities (Col 2:15); therefore, the peace Christ accomplished in their humiliation rules in our hearts and we no longer live in fear of the darkness they promise, always falsely, to save us from. So emboldened, we can risk living without calculating and self-protecting cynicism or contempt for weakness. We can risk treating others, especially those who cannot return our kindnesses, with generosity and compassion (Col 3:5-17). We can risk doing good, as it has been done for us.

The good we are to do is never spectacular. We do not have to change the world: we only have to witness to the fact that it has been and shall be changed, and is therefore already charged with God's grandeur. Jesus, of course, is the miracle-worker. He turns water to wine, liberates the captives, raises the dead. But, according to Matthew's Gospel, at the Last Judgment we are found faithful if we have simply fed the hungry, cared for the sick, and visited the prisoner. Hence, the truly Pentecostal life is, in Bonhoeffer's sense, "religionless," an "enlivening worldly godlessness" that in truth draws us ever closer to God,[21] a life "small enough to stop the violence."[22] In other words, we are called not so much to catch fire within Jerusalem as to gather ashes outside of Athens. And not only ashes. As Jane Liddell-King confesses at the end of her Setonian Prize–winning poem, "The Golden Calf," we also gather the fragments of the broken word for the sake of the broken world:

> and Moshe's face shines as the moon on the sea
> and touching the sand where the tablets of Adonai were broken
>   and scattered
>
> Aaron says to all of us together
> *Adonai Adonai*
> *ve-tiake lo yenake poked avon avot al banitn ve-al betiei vanim*
> *al shileshitn*
> *ve-al ribeitn*
>
> Shema Yisrael
> Adonai Elohenu Adonai Echad
>
> it will take years to pick up these pieces.[23]

Liturgically, we do this work each week at the Lord's table. And unlike Phocion's widow, who ingested her disgraced husband's ashes, making her body his tomb; and unlike the Israelites, who drank the slags of Aaron's idol after Moses ground it to power; we eat and drink the eucharistic bread and wine, "the holy food and drink of new and unending life in Christ," and find ourselves consumed with feeding others, especially those eaten up by the corrupt powers of the world, sent out in peace to make peace with those who have known only violence. Gathered in worship, we look to God and see that Christ's face is turned toward those who have been left out or sent away. Scattered in mission, we become Christ's nearness to them—his presence, his attention, his voice, his touch. And in this way, and in this way only, we take part in his work of renewing not only the city but also the face of the whole earth.

10

More Than Many Sparrows

Ordinary Time

Man is therefore indispensable to God's plan or, to be more
exact, man is nothing other than the divine plan within being.
Emmanuel Levinas

Do not be afraid; you are of more value than many sparrows.
Matthew 10:31

The Power to create is generative, yes. But it is so as a lavish welcome
into being, a communication of Life that rings out with the joy of Divine
Life itself. Come in, the Voice says; come home; welcome!
Katherine Sonderegger

The Mystery of Christ, Ordinary Time, and the Great Ordeal

Liturgically, the time from Advent, which opens the cycle, to
Epiphany, and then the time from Ash Wednesday to Pentecost,
is extraordinary. These high holy seasons anticipate and celebrate the dramatic events of Christ's redemptive mission, sum-
moning us to times of fasting in anticipation of his birth and in
preparation for his death, and to times of feasting in celebration
of his baptism, transfiguration, resurrection, and ascension as
the Spirit-baptized, Spirit-baptizing redeemer of all things. But
the bulk of the liturgical year, thirty-three or thirty-four weeks,
is given to "ordinary time."[1] This season, or interruption in the
seasons, reminds us that God's work is not limited to dramatic
events. The Spirit Christ pours out on us remains with us even in

what we mistake for "throwaway" moments. But it also reminds us that Christ's life and death are necessary to save us from evil and what evil has done to us and our world. Life is marked at every turn by suffering, and nothing is more ordinary than death. The liturgy of Ordinary Time reminds us that we are caught up in the unfolding of the mystery of the apocalypse. The Christian life, therefore, is not only a life of gratitude and obedience but also a life of lamentation and dissent. Creation groans and we groan because nothing is yet as it should be.

Martin Buber, in a letter to a Christian friend, admits respect for Jesus' teaching and sympathy for his character but insists he cannot hail him as savior because the world is so unmistakably unredeemed. "I am not at all capable of believing in a Messiah who already came so many years ago, because I have too profound a sense of the world's unredeemedness." The last thing he wants, he says, is "to live in an unredeemed world with a 'redeemed' soul." In Buber's view, redemption is the making right of all wrongs, the bringing to full flourishing of all creation at once and forever. "Redemption is a transformation of the whole of life from its very bottom, of the life of all individuals and all communities. The world is unredeemed—don't you feel that, as I do, in every drop of blood?"[2]

Twenty-five years earlier, in a letter to the poet and playwright Franz Werfel, Buber remarked that what bothers him most about Christian theology is the suggestion that God does not need us, and that we do not need to take responsibility for what happens in the world. God waits on us, Buber says, longing to rest upon us as he rested upon Jesus at his baptism: "My son, in all of the prophets I waited for you . . . You are my rest."[3]

> And how could I possibly grasp what the Christians find so easy to grasp, that God does not need me! That I have been made for a plaything and not for a perfecting . . . No, my friend, nothing is imposed upon us by God; everything is expected of us. And you rightly say: It lies within our choice whether we want to live the true life: in order to perfect him

in our uniqueness. But according to the Christian teaching, which has turned the meaning and the ground of Jesus upside down, nothing lies within our choice; rather, everything depends on whether or not we have been elected. Our teaching is: It is not a question of whether He has elected me, but that I have elected Him. For it is truly not His business to elect and to reject. Whereas the teaching that calls itself Christian hinders men, by referring them to divine grace, from making that decision which Jesus proclaimed.[4]

Although Buber misunderstands Christian doctrine, he understands perfectly well what is wrong with the teachings some Christians had presented to him. He rightly denounces the idea that believers can disregard the notrightness of the world. And he rightly affirms the need for believers to commit themselves to working with God against all that has gone wrong. We need, as he says, to elect God. And precisely because we love God, we should be constantly in anguish—grieved at the wretchedness of our condition and angered by every injustice, however slight.

The Whirlwind and the Burning Bush

Buber's essay on Job argues that there is a "great inner dialectic" to the poem, which sets four views of God in contrast. First, the prologue presents a God who is unworthy of the name, a God who acts rashly and allows cruelty for no reason. Second, the friends present in their rebukes of Job a God who establishes and upholds a flawless system of retribution, one in which those who suffer have sinned and so earned their suffering. Third, Job in his complaints and protests presents a self-contradicting and capricious God who violates his own justice and deals "crookedly" with his creatures. Fourth, God, answering Job, presents himself in revelation, both abolishing and fulfilling Job's expectations. "The way of his poem," Buber argues, "leads from the first view to the fourth." The view of the prologue is "ironical and unreal." The view of the friends is true only as an abstraction. God's view, of course, is true, but is given only in response to Job's grievances and accusations, which are "the negative of truth." At last, God justifies Job and chastises Job's friends, sending them home with a word of promise: "And my servant Job shall pray for you" (Job 42:8). Buber observes that God names Job "servant" four times in the epilogue, suggesting that in this way God regards Job, "the faithful rebel," as an equal to Abraham, Moses, David, Isaiah, and the suffering servant in Isaiah.[5]

Susan Schreiner has shown that Calvin was endlessly troubled both by Job's charges against God and by God's apparent irrationality and arbitrariness. "In short," she says, "the sovereignty of Job's God scared even Calvin."[6] Yet, he preached more than 150 sermons on Job, largely in defense of the doctrine of providence. Calvin defended the view of the friends, arguing that their failures were mostly pastoral and rhetorical, not theological. They were, on the whole, right to defend God's justice but wrong to claim that it is always immediate and discernable.[7] As Elihu understands better than either Job or his friends, God's sovereignty is certain, but often if not always inscrutable and mysterious. Thus, in Calvin's estimation, Elihu's anger against Job was entirely necessary and justified. Technically, Job is right: his sufferings are not punishment for his sins. But he handles his case before God badly, and foolishly imagines that because he has not sinned, he is therefore just before God.[8] Job, for Calvin, is not a faithful rebel, but a man losing faith because of his rebellion.

In Calvin's theology, the interplay of revelation and hiddenness matches the dialectic of nature and history. God "hid his face" in history but nature remained the "face of God." But in his sermons on the whirlwind speech, Calvin contends that humans are ignorant with respect to all the works of God, whether natural or historical. God, in other words, is hidden even in his revelation and revealed even in his hiddenness. And in any case, humans remain without excuse.[9] For his part, Buber holds that God's answer to Job is in truth a reply—a personal, intimate response. "God offers Himself to the sufferer who, in the depths of his despair, keeps to God with his refractory complaint; He offers Himself to him as an answer." Thus, in Buber's reading, what matters is not so much what God says about nature as the fact that he comes near to Job to say it. But I find this reading of the whirlwind speech almost as dissatisfying as Calvin's.

In response to God's thunderous speech, which was hardly an answer at all, Job crumbles in subjugation, and perhaps also submission, confessing his sins and owning his utter insignificance in the face of divine ascendancy (Job 42:1-6):

> "I know that you can do all things,
> and that no purpose of yours can be thwarted.
> 'Who is this that hides counsel without knowledge?'
> Therefore I have uttered what I did not understand,
> things too wonderful for me, which I did not know.
> 'Hear, and I will speak;
> I will question you, and you declare to me.'
>
> "I had heard of you by the hearing of the ear,
> but now my eye sees you;
> therefore I despise myself,
> and repent in dust and ashes."

Christians tend to ignore the fact that this prayer, at least on its face, makes no good sense. If Job's friends were wrong in what they claimed about the workings of divine justice, and if Job was right in what he said about God and about himself, as God says he was, then why does Job repent? And why does God seemingly reward Job for being right and threaten to punish the friends for being wrong? What is more, early in the story Job argues, against Bildad's insistence, that his innocence does not matter to God: "If I summoned him and he answered me, I do not believe that he would listen to my voice." How can the creature withstand the power of the creator? "If it is a contest of strength, he is the strong one! . . . Though I am innocent, my own mouth would condemn me; though I am blameless, he would prove me perverse" (Job 9:15-20). Is that not exactly what does happen, in the end?

Elie Wiesel is right: the end of Job is only apparently a happy one. Careful readers are left unnerved and disappointed. We know what has happened, and that what has happened is momentous. We know the telling of it is magnificent. But we know nothing more about why it has happened the way it has happened than we knew at first. Satan, who enticed God into the game at the beginning, makes no appearance at all in the ending. And we cannot help but be troubled by the fact that Job never learns what we, as readers of his story, know about that beginning. In Wiesel's words, "of all the injustices done to Job . . . the most humiliating, the most demeaning is the fact that never, never, does he learn the truth and the origin of his story . . . Job was entitled to know the truth. He never learned the truth."[10] God's response to Job's friends, which affirms Job's righteousness, seems entirely at odds with his response to Job, which only deepens Job's confusion and humiliation. So, Wiesel asks, why does God respond as he does? Perhaps because Job has done to God what Job's friends had done to Job? If they were guilty of assuming that all suffering is meaningful, then he was guilty of assuming suffering is always meaningless. Both alike reduced suffering to the theoretical. In a sense, then, Job was not so much a victim of injustice as a victim of his own thinking about justice. And in order to expose Job's errors, therefore, "God asks questions the way a pupil asks his master questions." And that is enough for Job. The question is, is it enough for us?

There is a way of reading Job that leads us to read our suffering, and the suffering of others, as vital and purifying. Nagai Takashi's memoir, *The Bells of Nagasaki*, provides an extreme example. In a funeral address given a few months after the explosion and in front of the destroyed Cathedral of the Assumption, Takashi attempted to make sense of the horror by declaring his city, "the only holy place in all Japan," a "pure lamb" slaughtered to expiate the sins of humanity. "In order to restore peace to the world it was not sufficient to repent. We had to obtain God's pardon through the offering of a great sacrifice."

How noble, how splendid was that holocaust of August 9, when flames soared up from the cathedral, dispelling the darkness of war and bringing the light of peace! In the very depth of our grief we reverently saw here something beautiful, something pure, something sublime. Eight thousand people, together with their priests, burning with pure smoke, entered into eternal life.

Takashi calls the surviving Japanese Christians to embrace the work of intercession and penitence. "As we walk in hunger and thirst, ridiculed, penalized, scourged, pouring with sweat and covered with blood, let us remember how Jesus Christ carried His cross to the hill of Calvary. He will give us courage." And in his closing lines, he refers to the words of Jesus and the words of Job from the prologue: "Blessed are those that mourn for they shall be comforted." "The Lord has given; the Lord has taken away. Blessed be the name of the Lord!"[11]

Someone has said the book of Job is a machine for generating endless and endlessly contradictory interpretations. In that way, this story proves to be more or less exactly like history itself, like our daily lives. We are interpreting creatures, which means we are bound to live not so much with what happens to us as with what we tell ourselves about what has happened to us. But we never know for sure the truth of it, at least not in a way that can be shared. Thus, for me, at least at this point in my life, the greatest power of the story of Job rests in what it does not say, in the gaps between the events and exchanges. In particular, I find it striking that God does not accept or respond in any way to Job's prayer of repentance. After Job has finished speaking, the narrator explains: "*After the* Lord *had spoken these words to Job*, the Lord said to Eliphaz the Temanite: 'My wrath is kindled against you and against your two friends; for you have not spoken of me what is right, as my servant Job has'" (Job 42:7). Why does God, why does the narrator, ignore what Job has said? And what does God praise in Job? He says Job has "spoken of me what is right." But what was right in what Job said? Was he right at first when he said God "crushes me with a tempest, and multiplies my wounds without cause" (Job 9:17)? Or was he right at last when he said "I know that you can do all things, and that no purpose of yours can be thwarted" (Job 42:1)? Rickie Moore argues that God celebrates not what Job has said, but how he has said it and to whom. What God praises, in other words, is the fact that Job *prays*.

> Job prays repeatedly during the course of his interaction with his friends, while they, on the other hand, are never seen addressing God a single time. They speak profusely about God, and they even speak about speaking to God, but only Job breaks out beyond the boundaries of inter-human dialogue to address God directly. In fact, Job is too direct, in another sense of the term, for the theological sensibilities of his friends. Indeed, this seems to be what sparks their dispute with Job in the first place.[12]

Moore takes issue with Gustavo Gutiérrez' too-neat distinction between talking about and talking to God: "Job is distinct from his friends not only in that he speaks to God and they do not, but also in that he dares to speak to God with a bold, confrontive and challenging directness which they reject on theological principle."[13] Unlike the friends, unlike Elihu, Job "prays through." And this is what makes him right again.

Other readings remain possible, of course. It is true that lament is a "form-shattering" experience, one that opens us up to the God who is without form but not void, the God who breaks all forms in order to make us whole. But this story suggests lamentation is true only if it rises into intercession. Tellingly, Job's restoration comes only after he prays for his friends. But that restoration is itself a new trouble. We read that "the LORD gave Job twice as much as he had before" (Job 42:10). But we feel in our guts, in our bones, that this "more" is not enough to make up for what Job had lost—not even close. And that dissatisfaction we feel at the end of this story, I am convinced, is purposeful. The drama is designed to fluster us and to frustrate us, to hurt us so we can know where we have been harmed and how we are harming others. A good reading of Job, then, is one that leaves us suspicious of what we have been told to accept as normal or common, especially when it is given the name of blessing, and one that frees us to question the meaning of the whirlwind. A good reading of Job is one that knows the story's place in Israel's history, and so realizes that God does not respond to Job's repentance because Job never should have offered it. Job himself is not a Jew, so he does not know what Israel has known from the beginning: true blessing comes only to those who contend with God and prevail. He never realizes that God is waiting, even after the restoration, for him to stand up and fight. And to fight not only for himself, although that is crucial, but to fight for others—including his friends who had been forced to bow before him as he had bowed before God.

Moses, a true Israelite, fought with God as his ancestors did and as his descendants did and do. At the burning bush, in his first encounter with the God of his father and his fathers, Moses hid his face, afraid to look at God (Exod 3:6). But the God of the burning bush, unlike the God of the whirlwind, calls Moses to stand (Exod 3:5). And later, at the summit of Sinai, Moses finally comes near to God, entering into the "devouring fire" (Exod 24:17), and speaks with God "face to face, as one speaks to a friend" (Exod 33:11). Later still, he sees and hears the glory of God, although he is warned: "I will make all my goodness pass before you, and will proclaim before you the name . . . [but] you cannot see my face; for no one shall see me and live" (Exod 33:19-20). This warning is an answer to Pharaoh's earlier threat against Moses: "Take care that you do not see my face again, for on the day you see my face you shall die" (Exod 10:28). Everything, literally everything, depends on the difference between that warning and that threat. And everything, literally everything, depends on us coming to know, as Elijah learned, that God is neither in the whirlwind nor in the fire (1 Kgs 19:11-12). The God who calls us to take off our sandals does so because he wants to wash our feet.

The Temptation of the Cross

In Leipzig, on the night of July 7, 1913, Franz Rosenzweig, one of Buber's close friends, almost converted to Christianity because of his conversation with two Christian friends, Eugen Rosenstock and Rudolf Ehrenberg. Benjamin Pollock argues that Rosenzweig was drawn to Christianity not because he was enthralled by the truth of Christian teaching or the sincerity of his friends' faith, but because he realized through their witness that he was responsible to join God in working for the redemption of the world. At first, he thought this required him to become a Christian. At last, he recognized that the Jewish people had a peculiar role to play in God's project, and that he, as a Jew, had to give himself to that work. Up to that point, he had felt that personal salvation required a radical denial of the world, a refusal to engage with misery and corruption. But that conversation freed him from the lie. And as his thought matured, he came to grasp more and more firmly that God purposes not only to reveal himself to the faithful but to work with them to make all things right. Thus, human beings—Jews in one way, Christians in another—must make a decision for God and for God's commitment to creation.[14]

This turn positioned Rosenzweig to see clearly the meaning of the Christian calling, and the need for Christians to keep their attention on Jesus, his teaching, his life and death:

> The historical Jesus must always take back from the ideal Christ the pedestal under his feet upon which his philosophical or nationalistic worshippers would like to set him, for an "idea" unites in the end with every wisdom and every self-conceit and confers upon them their own halo. But the historical Christ, precisely Jesus the Christ in the sense of the dogma, does not stand on a pedestal; he really walks in the marketplace of life and compels life to keep still under his gaze.[15]

When Christ is idealized, reimagined in abstraction from the story of Jesus in ways that serve any purpose or cause other than God's, the cross is reduced to a means by which the self is rescued out of the midst of existence and unburdened of all responsibilities for what happens in the world. And if the Christian life is construed in these terms, then lament and intercession are unintelligible, and praise turns out to be nothing but boasting. But, as Rosenzweig understood, the cross is a witness against what the world has done to us and what we have done to the world. This is why, as Bauerschmidt says, "Rather than ask why God wanted Jesus to *die* the way he did, we should ask why God wants Jesus to *live* the way he did and why this way of life led us to want to kill him." Dying, Jesus offers to God what he had offered throughout his life: "unconditional commitment to the cause of God's kingdom, complete openness to God and trust in the power of divine love, and a hunger and thirst for righteousness."[16] And that, exactly that, is what we are called to choose, to decide for. We have been assured that if we do make that choice, not once, but as often as needed, we will become more and more ourselves and so less and less willing to accept the way things are in and around us. Johannes Baptist Metz says this is what it means to be "poor in spirit."

> It is no accident that "poverty of spirit" is the first of the beatitudes. What is the sorrow of those who mourn, the suffering of the persecuted, the self-forgetfulness of the merciful, or the humility of the peacemakers—what are these if not variations of spiritual poverty? This spirit is also the mother of the three-fold mystery of faith, hope, and charity. It is the doorway through which we must pass to become authentic human beings. Only through poverty of spirit do we draw near to God; only through it does God draw near to us. Poverty of spirit is the meeting point of heaven and earth, the mysterious place where God and humanity encounter each other, the point where infinite mystery meets concrete existence.[17]

We are called, in Metz' phrase, to a "mysticism of open eyes," a way of caring unpossessively for others, trusting them with our fullest attention, so that the form of our life itself becomes an intercessory prayer.

Small Helplessnesses Make Us Maternal

Jesus' words, "Do not be afraid; you are of more value than many sparrows," are more often than not taken as a kindhearted, homespun reminder that everything in our lives, down to the minutest detail, is under God's gentle care. Calvin certainly takes it that way. But in the flow of the Gospel reading, Jesus' words take on an altogether different sense. Matthew 10, which those who follow the Revised Common Lectionary read during Ordinary Time, the third Sunday after Pentecost, recounts the sending of the Twelve on their apostolic mission to proclaim the happy news that God's government is soon to be established. Jesus instructs them to "cure the sick, raise the dead, cleanse the lepers, cast out demons" and to live without pretense or affectation. "You received without payment; give without payment. Take no gold, or silver, or copper in your belts, no bag for your journey, or two tunics, or sandals, or a staff." He reminds them of his intentions—"I have not come to bring peace, but a sword"—and he tells them in no uncertain terms that their allegiance to him will cost them their lives.

> See, I am sending you out like sheep into the midst of wolves; so be wise as serpents and innocent as doves. Beware of them, for they will hand you over to councils and flog you in their synagogues; and you will be dragged before governors and kings because of me, as a testimony to them and the Gentiles. . . . Brother will betray brother to death, and a father his child, and children will rise against parents and have them put to death; and you will be hated by all because of my name. But the one who endures to the end will be saved. When they persecute you in one town, flee to the next; for truly I tell you, you will not have gone through all the towns of Israel before the Son of Man comes. (Matt 10:16-18, 21-23)

In a word, Jesus calls the disciples to take up his cross. And, as Bonhoeffer sees, the cross is his sword. "It creates division. The son against the father, the daughter against the mother, the household against its head, and all that for the sake of God's kingdom and its peace—that is the work of Christ on earth."[18] It is in this context that Jesus offers his word of assurance:

> So have no fear of them; for nothing is covered up that will not be uncovered, and nothing secret that will not become known. What I say to you in the dark, tell in the light; and what you hear whispered, proclaim from the housetops. Do not fear those who kill the body but cannot kill the soul; rather fear him who can destroy both soul and body in hell. Are not two sparrows sold for a penny? Yet not one of them will fall to the ground apart from your Father. And even the hairs of your head are all counted. So do not be afraid; you are of more value than many sparrows. (Matt 10:26-31)

Sparrows were sold in the market cheaply as food for the poorest of the poor. In saying that God sees each one that falls, Jesus reminds his disciples that they are seen and known by God. But this is a strange comfort: we are seen and known by the God of the poor, the God who is poor; and this means we will not be kept from pain and loss. Just the opposite, in fact. The more we become like him, the more we will suffer and surrender. But this will not be done in vain: everything, truly everything, will be set right as our reward. We know Buber's prayer for "a transformation of the whole of life from its very bottom, of the life of all individuals and all communities"[19] will be answered and more than answered. In the meantime, as we await that setting-right, we give ourselves unstintingly to the care of "the least of these," knowing that God is present to us in them and to them in us. Together, their need and our service bears witness against what has become of the world—against violence and exploitation, greed and idolatry, negligence and ingratitude. Christians, then, learn in Ordinary

Time to live as Christ did: never confusing prosperity for blessing or scarcity for penalty; content with whatever God has given; desperate in the face of calamity and injustice; mourning, but not as those who have no hope; confident that God's hiddenness is for our good.

The poet Deborah Digges limns this way of life wonderfully in her extraordinary poem, "Vesper Sparrows." After the opening lines, in which she celebrates watching sparrows "sheathe themselves mid-air / shut wings and ride the light's poor spine," even if at last they "touch down in gutters, in the rainbowed / urine of suicides, just outside Bellevue's walls," she turns to what she has learned about death. "The first time I saw the inside of anything / alive, a downed bird opened cleanly / under my heel. I knelt / to watch the spectral innards shine and quicken, / the heart-whir magnify." From that time, she found herself brought face to face with death, until it became ordinary—"I have identified so many times that sudden / earnest spasm of the throat in children." And slowly, she realizes she is being led to embrace her smallness, her frailty: "I've read small helplessnesses make us maternal." And she realizes, wonderfully, that it is that very same small helplessness that the sparrows embody perfectly:

> Even the sparrows feel it,
> nesting this evening in traffic lights.
>
> They must have remembered, long enough to mate,
> woods they've never seen,
>
> but woods inbred up the long light of instinct,
> the streaked siennas of a forest floor
>
> born now into the city,
> the oak umbers, and the white tuft
>
> of tail feathers like a milkweed meadow
> in which their song, as Burroughs heard it,

could be distinguished:
come-come-where-where-all-together-
down-the-hill . . .
here, where every history is forfeited,

where the same names of the different dead greet
each other and commingle

above the hospital's heaps of garbage.
From the ward windows, fingerprinted,

from the iron-grated ledges,
hundreds flock down for the last feed of the day

and carry off into the charitable dusk what
cannot be digested.[20]

Those last lines are perfect, just as sparrows are perfect. And our
lives can be perfect in this way, too.

Conclusion

What, then, shall we say in response to these things? If God is for us, who can be against us? He who did not spare his own Son, but gave him up for us all—how will he not also, along with him, graciously give us all things?

Romans 8:31-32 NIV

But what if his flesh felt more than ours, knew each breath was a gift, and thus saw beyond each instant into all others?

Mary Karr

When God draws near, the glow of our humanity shines even more brightly before us.

Johannes Baptist Metz

Aesthetic Christology, at least as I have attempted it, is formed by and emerges from a spirited, searching conversation between theology and art, guided by the themes of the liturgical year. It assumes an "inner kinship" between art and theology, and it assumes that this kinship is revelatory and instructive. But it is worth asking outright: Why and how is that kinship effected? And why and how does it affect us? Natalie Carnes concludes her work on icons and iconoclasm with a provoking question, one which urges us to think carefully about the nature of creation at its depths, in its relation to God: "Who is to say where and in what way and by which images God might once again come to us, bearing unanticipated forms of divine presence?"[1] Icons, she says, share a unique relationship to Christ, the true image of God. But this need not mean they are the only images that bear God's presence or lay bare an absence that calls for his presence. God "might once again come to us" in *any* image—our faces, the surface of the sea, a murmuration, a ghost apple, this photograph, that coin, your child's scribbled drawings. And this is so because creation is accomplished in what happened with Jesus of Nazareth. As St. Maximus recognized with remarkable clarity, the mystery of creation is by God's decision identical with and so inseparable from the mystery of the incarnation. In Christ, the divine and the human, creator and created, are drawn into an inexhaustible intimacy, a fully realized and transcendent mutuality. The event of that communion, Christians believe, is what accomplishes redemption.

According to Christian dogma, Jesus is capable of accomplishing this redemption because he is "Son," and makes room for us in his relation to the one he calls "Father." And this redemption has the character it has because of the nature of the Son's relation to the Father through the Spirit. As Williams explains in an outstanding essay on the trinitarian theology of St. John of the Cross,

> The single life of the Godhead is the going-out from self-identity into the other; that cannot be a closed mutuality (for then the other would be only the mirror of the same); the love of one for other must itself open on to a further otherness if it is not to return to the same; and only so is the divine life "as a whole" constituted as love (rather than mutual reinforcement of identity). If so, the designation of both Spirit and divine essence as love makes sense: it is the Spirit as excess of divine love that secures the character of God-as-such.[2]

This, then, is the wonder of the gospel: what is true of God's life with God is true of God's life with us, because all that he is he shares without reserve or stint with creation. Thanks to the Spirit, the Son is "the cause of joy" in the Father, and the Son takes joy in the Father. But God's life does not close in on itself. The Father delights in us just as he delights in the Son, and Jesus desires for us to enjoy the very same gladness, the very same satisfaction, he enjoys as the divinely beloved. God shares that with us in and through the happenings of Jesus' life. As Williams says in his recent Christology, *Christ the Heart of Creation*, "Creation is healed and restored to itself not by a supplement or an interruption but by an opening into its own depths of connection with the creative act. Christ is the event of that opening, revealing the Creator as the guarantor of creation's integrity, the point upon which finite form converges in beauty."[3]

We need to be brought back to this truth again and again: in the way that he lives and dies, Christ reveals that God's being is entirely other-oriented. This is the unbelievably good news that Easter announces: God's passion is and has always been only for us, not for himself. And Scripture declares it without equivocation: he did not withhold his own Son, but gave him up for us, and through him gave us all things (Rom 8:32). God made all that is—and redeemed it from the evil that threatened it—for our glory (1 Cor 2:7). To put it bluntly, then, there is no selfishness in God, no vanity or narcissism, no jealousy or envy, no domination or subjugation. God's life is simply gift from beginning to end. And creation exists and consists within that endless, boundless giving, receiving and reciprocation of gift.

Christ does more than merely show that it is true: he makes it true for us. He is, as Williams says, "the event of that opening," guaranteeing our full flourishing and assuring our humanity against any violation or loss. As Johannes Baptist Metz says, "When God draws near, the glow of our humanity shines even more brightly before us. God brightens our true greatness as human beings."[4] Each person and each thing that exists consists only in and through him and his sustaining intercession. And Jesus has been given the name above every name because he secures the integrity and viability of every name and everything that can be named.

Because creation exists in this relation to God, art and our appreciation of it, as well as theology, answer, and question, one another. And in the back-and-forth of conversation, they illuminate and inform one another. Mary Karr had always known that poetry saved her life. But looking back on her childhood in the light of her conversion, she realized that poetry could save her life just because it was eucharistic:

> I was a lonely, weird little kid, and for me poetry was eucharistic. The fact that another person felt the way I felt, as lonely, or sad, or scared, was so comforting to me, and I was so hungry for it. It was as if I could eat the poems, like they went into my body. That's what I mean by eucharistic: somebody else's passion, suffering, comes into your body and changes you.[5]

Her story underscores a fundamental truth: what Christ accomplished for creation matters not only for bread and wine, not only for bodies and souls, but also for art. We are called to "discern his body" wherever and however it appears to us.

Of course, as the framing of Carnes' question reminds us, our redemption, and so art's redemption, is not yet realized. We are changing: we are not yet changed. The opening Christ has made is ours only in hope, and "hope that is seen is not hope" (Rom 8:24). This is why we need him to come to us again and again, to grace us in ways that make it possible for us to remain faithful, to stay in the yoke with him. And he does this, as Carnes suggests, by presenting himself to us as he did to the disciples on their way home to Emmaus—at the right time, in the fullness of each time, in just the way we need to meet him. Art's redemption depends on us, and our "manifestation" as "sons and daughters," just as the whole creation does. So, it is fitting that Christ comes to us not only in "these creatures of bread and wine" and the faces of the poor, but also in our stories and songs and dances. What Carnes says of images, secular and sacred, is true of quite literally everyone and everything—not because creation is divine, but because Christ, the Creator, is divinely, personally free to be with us in the manner that is best for us. "The word of God is not bound" (2 Tim 2:9 AKJV). Hence, God's blessing may come to us in curses, whether ours or another's. And even irreverent or blasphemous films (or novels or paintings or plays or poems or photographs or songs) may prove somehow to be good for us. In the words of Hopkins' famous poem, kingfishers, thanks to Christ, sometimes catch fire, the just man sometimes justices, and the self sometimes "goes itself"—suddenly, magnificently alive, grateful for being, ready to face whatever comes. And that transfiguration, however fleeting, is a sign of what God has attained for us in Christ, as well as a reminder that both art and theology, in their myriad manifestations, are always capable of more than we can imagine—capable, in fact, of the infinite.

A worthwhile Christology, then, gives us some sense of Christ's capacity to be "all in all." And like good art, it surprises us in ways that leave us all at once disturbed and wondering. As I was writing this conclusion, I encountered Otto Dix's lithographs for the first time, and the frankness of his representations of Christ impressed on me something of the tense physicality of Jesus' presence and the starkness of his moods. In one image, Jesus leans toward a perturbed Simon Peter, touching him with an almost primal tenderness. Peter, for his part, remains seated, still grasping his nets awkwardly, eyeing Jesus with blatant suspicion. In another image, Christ faces his abusers, his own face terribly disfigured, while they mock him maniacally. But in Dix's representation of the temptations, Jesus is shown with his face turned away from a monstrous Satan. And the same is true of Christ's entry into Jerusalem: Dix's Jesus seems exhausted, overtaxed, angry. Considering these images, it is worth remembering that whenever Jesus is represented to us, we see no one other than God, although he can be represented only in his humanity.[6] The invisible, ineffable divinity of the Word can be known only in "the form of a slave." But this is not a scandal—at least not for God. God is happy to be imaged in us and by us and through the things we make. No doubt, iconoclasm is necessary; but never for God's sake. And to say that God is happy to be known as a human is a reminder that we can accept our creatureliness, our "transcendental neediness," as a gift.[7]

Dix's lithographs also remind us that the depths of Jesus' humanity, and so the depths of all creation, remain always inexhaustible, unfathomable, even in moments of disclosure. The form of Christ's life, and so the form of all lives—including the lives of the characters we make in our stories, in our poems, in our paintings—is always stranger, more superb and outlandish, than we could ever anticipate or explicate. Dix's art, like any good art, as well as any good theology, draws our attention to the reality of the story of Jesus in such a way that we can sense something of his incomprehensible otherness as well as his immeasurable goodness, permitting us to brush up against the eccentricity of God. In a word, Dix's representations of Christ are touching, but leave the impression that Jesus is "touched." And that impression, I believe, is the mark of creative and creaturely authenticity.

Bearing all that in mind, I want to end this last chapter the same way I ended the first—with a poem, which, at the risk of sounding trite, is in effect an irreverent responsive prayer to an irreverent and seemingly unresponsive God. This, I believe, is a fitting doxology for the God of the gospel, precisely because it seems so out of line:

> Oh the nonsense and madness of God
> *Gloria Patri**
> whose thoughts are not our thoughts
> *et Filio**
> whose ways are always only strange and unheroic
> *et Spiritui Sancto**
> Your judgments disenchant us
> *Sicut erat in principio**
> and you ever live to confound our aspirations
> *et nunc**
> To you belongs all weakness, shame, and infamy
> *et semper**
> now if not forever
> *et in sæcula sæculorum**
> through Jesus Christ our Lord
> *Amen.*

Notes

Introduction

1 David Bentley Hart, "The Gospel according to Melpomene: Reflections on Rowan Williams's *The Tragic Imagination*," *Modern Theology* 34, no. 2 (2018): 220–34 (221).

2 Thomas Merton, *No Man Is an Island* (New York: Harcourt & Brace, 1955), 239.

3 George Pattison, "Idol or Icon? Some Principles of an Aesthetic Christology," *Journal of Literature and Theology* 3, no. 1 (1989): 1–15 (9).

4 Garth Greenwell, "Making Meaning: Against 'Relevance' in Art," *Harper's Magazine*, November 2020, https://harpers.org/archive/2020/11/making-meaning-garth-greenwell/.

5 David Jones, *Epoch and Artist* (London: Faber and Faber, 1959), 100.

6 David Jones, *The Anathemata* (London: Faber and Faber, 1952), 49.

7 Originally published as "First and Last" in *Fare Forward*, September 30, 2020, http://farefwd.com/index.php/2020/09/30/first-and-last/.

1 | Painting a True Christ

1 Rowan Williams, "Grace, Necessity, and Imagination: Catholic Philosophy and the Twentieth Century Artist, Lecture 4: God and the Artist," Clark Lectures, Trinity College, Cambridge, March 3, 2005, no. 4.

2 Geoffrey Hill, "Poetry as 'Menace' and 'Atonement,'" *University of Leeds Review* 21 (1978): 66–88 (67).

3 Rowan Williams, "The Bible Today: Reading and Hearing," Larkin-Stuart Lecture, Trinity and Wycliffe Colleges, Toronto, April 16, 2007.

4 George Steiner, *Real Presences* (New York: Open Road, 2013), 139–40.

5 Steiner, *Real Presences*, 143.

6 Rowan Williams, "A Conversation with Rowan Williams," interview by John F. Deane, *Image* 80 (2014), https://imagejournal .org/article/conversation-rowan-williams/.

7 Description available online at The Criterion Channel website: https://www.criterionchannel.com/babette-s-feast.

8 Nick Ripatrazone, "*Mariette in Ecstasy*: Revisiting Ron Hansen's Outré, Erotic Catholic Novel, Twenty-Five Years Later," *The Paris Review*, November 22, 2016, https://www.theparisreview.org/blog/ 2016/11/22/mariette-in-ecstasy/.

9 Ron Hansen, *Mariette in Ecstasy* (New York: HarperCollins, 1991), 9.

10 Hansen, *Mariette in Ecstasy*, 159.

11 Matt Zoller Seitz, "'All Things Shining': The Films of Terrence Malick: *Badlands*," originally published on Moving Image Source, a publication of Museum of the Moving Image, May 11, 2011, video, 10:10, https://www.youtube.com/watch?v=NYfrI7EiXsU.

12 Makoto Fujimura, "Refractions 33: Georges Rouault—the First 21st Century Artist," October 17, 2009, https://www .makotofujimura.com/writings/refractions-georges-rouault/.

13 Hans W. Frei, *The Identity of Jesus Christ: The Hermeneutical Bases of Dogmatic Theology* (Eugene, Ore.: Wipf & Stock, 1997), 84.

14 Graham Greene, *The Power and the Glory* (New York: Penguin, 1991), 22.

15 Greene, *Power and the Glory*, 210.

16 Greene, *Power and the Glory*, 219.

17 Greene, *Power and the Glory*, 206.

18 Robert W. Jenson, "Christ as Culture 2: Christ as Art," *International Journal of Systematic Theology* 6, no. 1 (2004): 69–76.

19 Karl Rahner, "The Theology of the Symbol," in *Theological Investigations*, vol. 4 (London: Darton, Longman & Todd, 1966), 221–52 (222).

20 Karl Rahner, "Poetry and the Christian," in *Theological Investigations*, 4:357–67 (359).

21 St. John of Damascus, *Three Treatises on the Divine Images*, trans. Andrew Louth (Crestwood, N.Y.: St. Vladimir's Seminary, 2003), 3–6.

22 St. John of Damascus, *Three Treatises*, 6.

23 St. John of Damascus, *Three Treatises*, 7–8.

2 | All Things Beautiful in His Time

1 Karl Rahner, "The Festival of the Future of the World," in *Theological Investigations*, vol. 7 (London: Darton, Longman & Todd, 1971), 181–85 (183).

2 Mark C. Taylor, "Time's Struggle with Space: Kierkegaard's Understanding of Temporality," *Harvard Theological Review* 66, no. 3 (1973): 311–29 (329). See also Paul Ricoeur, *Time and Narrative*, vol. 1 (Chicago: University of Chicago Press, 1984).

3 Christian Wiman, *My Bright Abyss: Meditation of a Modern Believer* (New York: Farrar, Straus and Giroux, 2013), 128.

4 See Chris E. W. Green, *The End Is Music: A Companion to Robert W. Jenson's Theology* (Eugene, Ore.: Cascade, 2018).

5 Andrey Tarkovsky, *Sculpting in Time: Reflections on the Cinema*, trans. Kitty Hunter-Blair (Austin: University of Texas Press, 1989), 38, 118–19.

6 He suggests a metaphorical range for these pressures—"brook, spate, river, waterfall, ocean"—which flow at various intensities.

7 Tarkovsky, *Sculpting in Time*, 114.

8 Tarkovsky, *Sculpting in Time*, 43.

9 David Roark, "Terrence Malick and the Christian Story," RogerEbert.com, March 10, 2016, https://www.rogerebert.com/features/terrence-malick-and-the-christian-story.

10 Martin Laird, "Under Solomon's Tutelage: The Education of Desire in the *Homilies on the Song of Songs*," *Modern Theology* 18, no. 4 (2002): 507–25.

11 *The New World* (2005) and *A Hidden Life* (2019) are a pair and belong to a distinct project, although many of the same themes appear in them, as well.

12 Paula Fredriksen, "Augustine on God and Memory," in *Obliged by Memory: Literature, Religion, Ethics; A Collection of Essays Honoring Elie Wiesel's Seventieth Birthday*, ed. Steven T. Katz

and Alan Rosen (Syracuse, N.Y.: University of Syracuse Press, 2006), 131–38 (134).

13 Hannah Arendt, *Love and Saint Augustine*, ed. Joanna Vecchiarelli Scott and Judith Chelius Stark (Chicago: University of Chicago Press, 1996), 50–51.

14 Arendt, *Love and Saint Augustine*, 49, 57.

15 Peter J. Leithart, *Shining Glory: Theological Reflections on Terrence Malick's "Tree of Life"* (Eugene, Ore.: Cascade, 2013), 3.

16 See Steven Chase, "Recollection," in *The New Westminster Dictionary of Christian Spirituality*, ed. Philip Sheldrake (Louisville, Ky.: Westminster John Knox, 2005), 525–26. Roger Ebert's description is from Ebert, "The Blink of a Life, Enclosed by Time and Space," review of *The Tree of Life*, RogerEbert.com, June 1, 2011, https://www.rogerebert.com/reviews/the-tree-of-life-2011.

17 Leithart, *Shining Glory*, 66.

18 T. S. Eliot, "The Waste Land," lines 307–8, in *The Waste Land and Other Poems*, ed. Christopher B. Ricks (Orlando, Fla.: Harcourt, Brace, 1997), 36.

19 Donald MacKinnon, "Some Notes on the Irreversibility of Time," in *Explorations in Theology*, vol. 5 (Eugene, Ore.: Wipf & Stock, 2012), 90–98 (97).

20 Karl Rahner, "Thoughts on the Theology of Christmas," in *Theological Investigations*, vol. 3 (London: Darton, Longman and Todd, 1967), 24–34.

21 W. H. Auden, *For the Time Being: A Christmas Oratorio*, ed. Alan Jacobs (Princeton, N.J.: Princeton University Press, 2013), 65.

22 See, for example, John Swinton, *Dementia: Living in the Memories of God* (Grand Rapids: Eerdmans, 2012).

23 Auden, *For the Time Being*, 64.

3 | The Name above All Names

1 Richard Slotkin, *Regeneration through Violence: The Mythology of the American Frontier, 1600–1860* (Norman: University of Oklahoma Press, 1973), 269.

2 Richard Slotkin, *Gunfighter Nation: The Myth of the Frontier in Twentieth-Century America* (New York: Macmillan, 1992), 499–500.

3 Slotkin, *Gunfighter Nation*, 512.

4 Slotkin, *Gunfighter Nation*, 654.

5 Slotkin, *Gunfighter Nation*, 533.

6 Slotkin, *Gunfighter Nation*, 657.

7 David Milch, "Television's Great Writer, David Milch," MIT Communications Forum, 2006, video, February 17, 2016.

https://techtv.mit.edu/videos/16086-television-s-great-writer
-david-milch-mit-communications-forum.

8   As Slotkin (*Gunfighter Nation*, 505) says, in his occult style, "The hunter's violence, markedly sexual in its symbolic character, brings him into communion with the goddess of this world, the wilderness. Yet the violence itself and the consequent initiation into another identity violate the norms of European culture and of Christian morality and moralized sexuality. To accept whole-heartedly the wilderness marriage and Eucharist is to lose one's white soul; to hold back is to fail in America as an American."

9   Mark Twain, "Fenimore Cooper's Literary Offenses," available online at http://xroads.virginia.edu/~Hyper/HNS/Indians/offense .html.

10 Kristin Kobes Du Mez, *Jesus and John Wayne: How White Evangelicals Corrupted a Faith and Fractured a Nation* (New York: Liveright, 2020), 12–15.

11 Slotkin, *Gunfighter Nation*, 519–20.

12 Andrew Louth, *Introducing Eastern Orthodox Theology* (Downers Grove, Ill.: InterVarsity, 2013), 129.

13 Maximus and Chrysologus, quoted in Philip H. Pfatteicher, *Journey into the Heart of God: Living the Liturgical Year* (New York: Oxford University Press, 2013), 115, 120.

14 Eugene Vodolazkin, *Laurus*, trans. Lisa C. Hayden (London: Oneworld, 2015), 146.

15 Vodolazkin, *Laurus*, 199.

16 Vodolazkin, *Laurus*, 350.

17 Will Arbery, *Heroes of the Fourth Turning* (New York: Samuel French, 2020), 81. Emphasis original unless noted.

18 Karl Rahner, "The Mature Christian," in *Theological Investigations*, vol. 21 (London: Darton, Longman & Todd, 1983), 113–29.

19 Samuel Wells, *Improvisation: The Drama of Christian Ethics* (Grand Rapids: Baker Academic, 2018), 24.

20 Rowan Williams, "A Curious Novel: Postmodernism and Holy Madness," TEDxOxBridge, July 5, 2016, video, 14:44, https:// www.youtube.com/watch?v=6MCB9JuLFzo.

4 | God's Scars

1   Erich Auerbach, *Mimesis: The Representation of Reality in Western Literature*, trans. Willard R. Trask (Princeton, N.J.: Princeton University Press, 1953), 11.

2   Auerbach, *Mimesis*, 3.

3   Auerbach, *Mimesis*, 9.

4   Auerbach, *Mimesis*, 11.

5   Auerbach, *Mimesis*, 10–11.
6   Auerbach, *Mimesis*, 17.
7   Auerbach, *Mimesis*, 15.
8   Aquinas, *ST* II.94.5.
9   Søren Kierkegaard, *Fear and Trembling/Repetition*, ed. and trans. Howard V. Hong and Edna H. Hong (Princeton, N.J.: Princeton University Press, 1983).
10   James Wetzel, "The Shrewdness of Abraham: Violence and Sexual Difference in a Paradigm of Monotheistic Faith," *Journal of Philosophy and Scripture* 3, no. 2 (2006): 25–30 (30).
11   Elie Wiesel, *Messengers of God: Biblical Portraits and Legends* (New York: Summit Books, 1976), 69–97.
12   André Neher, *The Exile of the Word: From the Silence in the Bible to the Silence of Auschwitz*, trans. David Maisel (Philadelphia: Jewish Publication Society of America, 1981), 217.
13   Elie Wiesel, *Ani Maamin: A Song Lost and Found Again* (New York: Random House, 1974), 42.
14   Wiesel, *Messengers of God*, 90–91.
15   Wiesel, *Messengers of God*, 93.
16   Wiesel, *Messengers of God*, 97.
17   Wiesel, *Messengers of God*, 76.
18   St. Augustine of Hippo, *City of God* 16.32, trans. Henry Bettenson (London: Penguin, 1984), 693–94.
19   Simone Weil, "*The Iliad*, or the Poem of Force," *Chicago Review* 18, no. 2 (1965): 5–30 (29).
20   R. S. Thomas, *Collected Poems 1945–1990* (London: J. M. Dent, 1993), 147.
21   Willie James Jennings, "Overcoming Racial Faith," *Divinity* 14, no. 2 (2015): 5–9, https://divinity.duke.edu/sites/divinity.duke.edu/files/divinity-magazine/DukeDivinityMag_Spring15.WEB_.compressed.pdf.
22   Toni Morrison, *Beloved* (New York: Random House, 2004), 175.
23   Morrison, *Beloved*, 295–96.

5 | Beauty Will Not Save the World

1   Maggie Ross, "By Our Wounds We Are Healed," *Voice in the Wilderness* (blog), February 11, 2008, https://ravenwilderness.blogspot.com/2008/02.
2   Debra Dean Murphy, "Alienated from Our Own Beauty," *Christian Century*, January 31, 2018, https://www.christiancentury.org/article/faith-matters/alienated-our-own-beauty.
3   Pope John Paul II, "Letter to Artists," April 4, 1999, http://www.vatican.va/content/john-paul-ii/en/letters/1999/documents/hf_jp-ii_let_23041999_artists.html.

4   Alexandr [Aleksandr] Solzhenitsyn, "Alexandr Solzhenitsyn—Nobel Lecture," NobelPrize.org, 1970, https://www.nobelprize.org/prizes/literature/1970/solzhenitsyn/lecture/.

5   Paul Evdokimov, *The Art of the Icon: A Theology of Beauty*, trans. Fr. Steven Bigham (Redondo Beach, Calif.: Oakwood, 1990).

6   Jacques Maritain, *Approaches to God* (Mahwah, N.J.: Paulist Press, 2015), 80.

7   Elaine Scarry, *On Beauty and Being Just* (Princeton, N.J.: Princeton University Press, 2001), 102–15.

8   For an example of such abuses, see David B. Dennis, *Inhumanities: Nazi Interpretations of Western Culture* (Cambridge: Cambridge University Press, 2012).

9   Ronald A. Sharp, "George Steiner: The Art of Criticism, No. 2," *The Paris Review* 137 (1995), https://www.theparisreview.org/interviews/1506/the-art-of-criticism-no-2-george-steiner.

10 Natalie Carnes, *Beauty: A Theological Engagement with Gregory of Nyssa* (Eugene, Ore.: Cascade, 2014), 62.

11 *The Book of Common Prayer* (New York: Oxford University Press, 2005), 264–69.

12 Carnes, *Beauty*, 66.

13 Carnes, *Beauty*, 79.

14 St. Augustine of Hippo, *Letters*, vol. 2 (83–130), trans. Wilfrid Parsons (Washington, D.C.: Catholic University of America Press, 1953), 381.

15 St. John of the Cross, *The Ascent of Mount Carmel* 1.4 and 3.21, in *The Collected Works of St. John of the Cross*, trans. Kieran Kavanaugh and Otilio Rodriguez (Washington, D.C.: Institute of Carmelite Studies, 2017), 125, 304.

16 Evdokimov, *Art of the Icon*, 60.

17 Misogyny and misanthropy are not essential to Christian belief and practice, even if they have marked much of the tradition. See Rosemary Radford Ruether, "Sexism and Misogyny in the Christian Tradition: Liberating Alternatives," *Buddhist-Christian Studies* 34, no. 1 (2014): 83–94.

18 Natalie Carnes, *Motherhood: A Confession* (Stanford, Calif.: Stanford University Press, 2020).

19 See Rowan Williams, "Plague as Metaphor," in *Plagues*, ed. Jonathan L. Heeney and Sven Friedemann (Cambridge: Cambridge University Press, 2017), 196–212.

20 M. Keith Booker, "The Dangers of Gullible Reading: Narrative as Seduction in García Márquez' *Love in the Time of Cholera*," *Studies in 20th & 21st Century Literature* 17, no. 2 (1993): 181–95 (191).

21 Fyodor Dostoevsky, *The Idiot*, trans. David McDuff (London: Penguin, 2004), 446.

22 Dostoevsky, *Idiot*, 94, 692–93.
23 Dostoevsky, *Idiot*, 91.
24 Quoted in Nicholas Berdyaev, *Dostoevsky*, trans. Donald Attwater (New York: Meridian, 1957), 59.
25 Dostoevsky, *Idiot*, 43.
26 Dostoevsky, *Idiot*, 95.
27 Dostoevsky, *Idiot*, 95.
28 Wendy Brenner, "Strange Beads," *Oxford American* 81, Summer 2013, https://www.oxfordamerican.org/magazine/item/222 -strange-beads.
29 Berdyaev, *Dostoevsky*, 119–20.
30 Jacques Maritain, *Creative Intuition in Art and Poetry* (New York: Pantheon-Bollingen Foundation, 1953), 167.
31 Fyodor Dostoevsky, *The Notebooks for "The Idiot,"* ed. Edward Wasiolek, trans. Katharine Strelsky (Mineola, N.Y.: Dover, 2017), 5.
32 Dostoevsky, *Notebooks for "The Idiot,"* 198.
33 Hermann Hesse, *My Belief: Essays on Life and Art*, edited by Theodore Ziolkowski, translated by Denver Lindley (New York: Farrar, Straus and Giroux, 1974), 86.
34 Edward Wasiolek, introduction to Dostoevsky, *Notebooks for "The Idiot,"* 15.
35 David Bentley Hart, *The Beauty of the Infinite: The Aesthetics of Christian Truth* (Grand Rapids: Eerdmans, 2003), 387. See also Hart, "The Gospel according to Melpomene," 220–34.
36 Maggie Smith, "Good Bones," in *Good Bones* (North Adams, Mass.: Tupelo, 2017), 79.
37 J. Todd Billings, *The End of the Christian Life: How Embracing Our Mortality Frees Us to Truly Live* (Grand Rapids: Brazos, 2020), 215.
38 Dostoevsky, *Idiot*, 47.
39 Dostoevsky, *Idiot*, 255.
40 Dostoevsky, *Idiot*, 269–70.
41 Rowan Williams, *Dostoevsky: Language, Faith, and Fiction* (Waco, Tex.: Baylor University Press, 2011), 51, 55.
42 Diane Oenning Thompson, "Problems of the Biblical Word in Dostoevsky's Poetics," in *Dostoevsky and the Christian Tradition*, ed. George Pattison and Diane Oenning Thompson (Cambridge: Cambridge University Press, 2001), 69–99.
43 Williams, *Dostoevsky*, 53.
44 Jonathan Jong, "Holbein's *Dead Christ*, Dostoevsky's *Idiot*, and Chalcedon's Christ," St Mary Magdalen School of Theology, June 26, 2020, https://www.theschooloftheology.org/posts/essay/holbein-dostoevsky-christ.
45 Cormac McCarthy, *The Road* (New York: Knopf, 2006), 241.

46 John W. de Gruchy, *Christianity, Art, and Transformation: Theological Aesthetics in the Struggle for Justice* (Cambridge: Cambridge University Press, 2001), 101.

6 | A Most Unspectacular Passion

1 Daniel Lapin, "Why Mel Owes One to the Jews," *Orthodoxy Today*.org, February 15, 2004, https://www.cbn.com/spirituallife/biblestudyandtheology/perspectives/passionmovie_rabbi.aspx.

2 Peggy Noonan, "It Is As It Was," *Wall Street Journal*, December 17, 2003, https://www.wsj.com/articles/SB122451994054350485.

3 John L. Allen Jr., "The Word from Rome," *National Catholic Reporter*, January 23, 2004, http://nationalcatholicreporter.org/word/word012304.htm.

4 Roger Ebert, review of *The Passion of the Christ*, RogerEbert.com, February 24, 2004, https://www.rogerebert.com/reviews/the-passion-of-the-christ-2004.

5 David Denby, "Nailed," review of *The Passion of the Christ*, *New Yorker*, February 22, 2004, https://www.newyorker.com/magazine/2004/03/01/nailed.

6 Mark Kermode, "Drenched in the Blood of Christ," review of *The Passion of the Christ*, *The Observer*, February 29, 2004, https://www.theguardian.com/theobserver/2004/feb/29/features.review7.

7 Ched Myers, "The Gospel of the Cross Confronts the Powers," in *Consuming Passion: Why the Killing of Jesus Really Matters*, ed. Simon Barrow and Jonathan Bartley (London: Darton, Longman & Todd, 2005), 61-73.

8 Mark Goodacre, "The Power of *The Passion*: Reacting and Overreacting to Gibson's Artistic Vision," in *Jesus and Mel Gibson's "The Passion of the Christ": The Film, the Gospels and the Claims of History*, ed. Kathleen E. Corley and Robert L. Webb (London: Continuum, 2004), 28-44.

9 Mark C. Taylor, "The Offense of Flesh," in *Mel Gibson's Bible: Religion, Popular Culture, and "The Passion of the Christ*," ed. Timothy K. Beal and Tod Linafelt (Chicago: University of Chicago Press, 2006), 139-52.

10 René Girard, "On Mel Gibson's *The Passion of the Christ*," *Anthropoetics: The Journal of Generative Anthropology* 10, no. 1 (Spring/Summer 2004), http://anthropoetics.ucla.edu/ap1001/rggibson/.

11 Girard, "On Mel Gibson's *The Passion of the Christ*."

12 Taylor, "Offense of Flesh," 151.

13 Girard, "On Mel Gibson's *The Passion of the Christ*."

14 Jeremy S. Begbie, "Beauty, Sentimentality and the Arts," in *The Beauty of God: Theology and the Arts*, ed. Daniel J. Treier, Mark

Husbands, and Roger Lundin (Downers Grove, Ill.: InterVarsity, 2007), 45–69.

15 John-Henry Westen, "Gibson Film Realistic Portrayal of Christ," review of *The Passion of the Christ*, *The Interim*, February 5, 2004, https://www.theinterim.com/issues/religion/gibson-film -realistic-portrayal-of-christ/.

16 J. D. Salinger, *The Catcher in the Rye* (New York: Little, Brown, 1979), 181.

17 Begbie, "Beauty, Sentimentality and the Arts," in Treier, Husbands, and Lundin, *Beauty of God*, 51.

18 Jean-Louis Chrétien, *The Ark of Speech*, trans. Andrew Brown (London: Routledge, 2004), 95.

19 Quoted in Chrétien, *Ark of Speech*, 95–96.

20 John Donne, "Good Friday, 1613. Riding Westward," Poetry Foundation, https://www.poetryfoundation.org/poems/44103/ good-friday-1613-riding-westward.

21 Chrétien, *Ark of Speech*, 101.

22 Robert W. Jenson, "God, Space, and Architecture," *Response* 8 (1967): 157–62.

23 Erich Auerbach, *Literary Language and Its Public in Late Latin Antiquity and in the Middle Ages*, trans. Ralph Manheim (Princeton, N.J.: Princeton University Press, 1965), 50–66.

24 Domenic Canonico, "Good Friday: Creation Always Exists in Darkness," *Church Life Journal*, March 29, 2018, https:// churchlifejournal.nd.edu/articles/good-friday-creation-always -exists-in-darkness/.

25 Karl Rahner, "Our Lord's Death on the Cross," in *Spiritual Exercises*, trans. Kenneth Baker (New York: Herder and Herder, 1965), 234–43 (239).

26 Karl Rahner, "See, What a Man!" in *Theological Investigations*, 7:136–39 (138).

27 Dietrich Bonhoeffer, *Ethics*, ed. Clifford J. Green, trans. Reinhard Krauss, Douglas W. Stott, and Charles C. West, *Dietrich Bonhoeffer Works* 6 (Minneapolis: Fortress, 2008), 84–85.

28 Rahner, "See, What a Man!" 138.

29 Franz Wright, "Arkansas Good Friday; III," *God's Silence* (New York: Knopf, 2008), 58.

7 | The End of All Endings

1 Jeremy Begbie, "The Sense of an Ending," The Veritas Forum, October 27, 2001, video, 1:37:15, http://www.veritas.org/sense-ending/.

2 Frank Kermode, *The Sense of an Ending: Studies in the Theory of Fiction* (Oxford: Oxford University Press, 2000), 26–27.

3   Kermode, *Sense of an Ending*, 27.
4   Kermode, *Sense of an Ending*, 2.
5   Kermode, *Sense of an Ending*, 193. Kermode, like Begbie and many others, takes the canonical placement of Revelation to be revelatory. But it is not included in Syriac Christian canons, and in others, it is placed just after the Gospels. See Robert W. Wall and Eugene E. Lemcio, eds., *The New Testament as Canon: A Reader in Canonical Criticism* (Sheffield, U.K.: JSOT Press, 1992); and Bruce M. Metzger, *The Canon of the New Testament: Its Origin, Development, and Significance* (Oxford: Clarendon, 1987).
6   Kermode, *Sense of an Ending*, 58.
7   N. T. Wright, "Reading Paul, Thinking Scripture," in *Scripture's Doctrine and Theology's Bible: How the New Testament Shapes Christian Dogmatics*, ed. Markus Bockmuehl and Alan J. Torrance (Grand Rapids: Baker Academic, 2005), 59–71 (60).
8   Stanley Hauerwas, "Character, Narrative, and Growth in the Christian Life," in *The Hauerwas Reader*, ed. John Berkman and Michael Cartwright (Durham, N.C.: Duke University Press, 2001), 221–54 (251–53).
9   Kermode, *Sense of an Ending*, 163.
10   Luke Timothy Johnson, *The Acts of the Apostles*, Sacra Pagina 5 (Collegeville, Minn.: Liturgical Press, 1992), 476.
11   Karl Rahner, "The Foundation of Belief Today," in *Theological Investigations*, vol. 16 (London: Darton, Longman & Todd, 1979), 3–23 (16).
12   Karl Rahner, "On the Spirituality of the Easter Faith," in *Theological Investigations*, vol. 17 (London: Darton, Longman & Todd, 1981), 8–15 (13).
13   Robert W. Jenson, *Systematic Theology*, vol. 1, *The Triune God* (New York: Oxford University Press, 2001), 194–205.
14   Karl Rahner, "Jesus' Resurrection," in *Theological Investigations*, 17:16–38 (21).
15   Jenson, *Systematic Theology*, 1:194–205.
16   Robert W. Jenson, *On Thinking the Human: Resolutions of Difficult Notions* (Grand Rapids: Eerdmans, 2003), 12–15.
17   John Updike, "Seven Stanzas at Easter," in *Telephone Poles and Other Poems* (London: Andre Deutsch, 1964), 72–73.
18   Maximus Confessor, *Ambigua ad Thomam* 5.50–58.
19   Maximus Confessor, *Opuscula theologica et polemica* 7 (emphasis added).
20   R. S. Thomas, "Suddenly," *Laboratories of the Spirit* (London: Macmillan, 1975), 32.

21 Franz Wright, "The Raising of Lazarus," Poetry Foundation, https://www.poetryfoundation.org/poetrymagazine/poems/ 58345/the-raising-of-lazarus.

22 Julian of Norwich, *Showings*, trans. James Walsh (Mahwah, N.J.: Paulist Press, 1978), 225.

23 John Updike, "Endpoint," *New Yorker*, March 9, 2009, https:// www.newyorker.com/magazine/2009/03/16/endpoint (emphasis added).

24 Barbara Herrnstein Smith, *Poetic Closure: A Study of How Poems End* (Chicago: University of Chicago Press, 2007), 13.

25 David Mamet, "They Think It's All Over: The Secret of a Great Ending—and the Movies That Are Lucky Enough to Have One," *The Guardian*, May 15, 2003, https://www.theguardian.com/ film/2003/may/16/artsfeatures.davidmamet.

26 André Neher, *They Made Their Souls Anew*, trans. David Maisel (Albany: State University of New York Press, 1990), 87–88.

8 | The Creative Gaze

1 This is a controversial story, made all the more controversial by recent revelations of O'Connor's racism. And so, it is tempting to avoid altogether her use of "nigger," which appears not only in the title of this story, but also in its dialogue (although it is never used by the narrator). But much like William Faulkner's stories, O'Connor's "The Artificial Nigger" is anti-racist in ways she herself was not and in ways she almost certainly did not intend. Arguably, then, the use of the abominable word is necessary, and not only for the sake of historical accuracy and artistic integrity. To censure the word would wrongly "protect" readers from confronting the possibility of their own subconscious racial prejudices and spites, especially if those are hidden behind a "white performative wokeness." See Paul Elie, "How Racist Was Flannery O'Connor?" *New Yorker*, June 15, 2020, https://www.newyorker.com/magazine/2020/06/22/how -racist-was-flannery-oconnor; and Paul Elie, "Confronting Flannery O'Connor's Racism: A Response to Angela Alaimo O'Donnell," *Commonweal*, August 12, 2020, https://www .commonwealmagazine.org/confront-facts-oconnor. See also Casey Cep, "William Faulkner's Demons," *New Yorker*, November 23, 2020, https://www.newyorker.com/magazine/2020/11/ 30/william-faulkners-demons.

2 Flannery O'Connor, "The Artificial Nigger," in *The Complete Stories* (New York: Farrar, Straus and Giroux, 1971), 268.

3 O'Connor, "Artificial Nigger," 269.

4 O'Connor, "Artificial Nigger," 269.

5 O'Connor, "Artificial Nigger," 270.

6 Flannery O'Connor, *The Habit of Being: Letters of Flannery O'Connor*, ed. Sally Fitzgerald (New York: Farrar, Straus and Giroux, 1988), 275.

7 Lucas E. Morel, "Bound for Glory: The Gospel of Racial Reconciliation in Flannery O'Connor's 'The Artificial Nigger,'" *Perspectives on Political Science* 34, no. 4 (2005): 202–10 (209).

8 O'Connor, "Parker's Back," in *The Complete Stories* (New York: Farrar, Straus and Giroux, 1971), 510–30 (530).

9 O'Connor, "Good Country People," in *The Complete Stories* (New York: Farrar, Straus and Giroux, 1971), 271–91 (291).

10 O'Connor, "Artificial Nigger," 269.

11 O'Connor, *Habit of Being*, 35.

12 As Elie's work has shown, O'Connor herself seems at least at times to have harbored some such feeling. But this story, whether she realized it or not, calls that feeling into the light, and exposes it for what it truly is.

13 I refer to the narrator with female pronouns, but in fact the narrator's identity is not revealed. In this case, if not always in O'Connor's stories, it is important to distinguish between the author's voice, the narrator's voices, and the voices of the characters.

14 O'Connor, "Artificial Nigger," 259.

15 O'Connor, "Artificial Nigger," 276.

16 O'Connor, "Artificial Nigger," 271.

17 It is telling, I believe, that the woman's afro "stood straight out from her head for about four inches all around," like a halo. As Deanna Ludwin ("O'Connor's Inferno: Return to the Dark Wood," *The Flannery O'Connor Bulletin* 17 [1988]: 11–39) explains, "the Black woman may be Nelson's Beatrice, willing to guide him out of his Hell via a car that will take him to the railroad station, but Mr. Head selfishly stops her intervention" (19). But of course, Beatrice appears to Dante not in hell, but in purgatory, which is yet another sign that Mr. Head has mistaken purgatory for hell. For the place of Francesca and Beatrice in Dante's poem, see Teodolinda Barolini, "Dante Alighieri," in *Women and Gender in Medieval Europe: An Encyclopedia*, ed. Margaret Schaus (New York: Routledge, 2006), 190–92.

18 O'Connor, "Artificial Nigger," 272.

19 *The Divine Comedy of Dante Alighieri*, vol. 3, *Paradiso*, trans. John D. Sinclair (London: Bodley Head, 1946), 485.

20 Gilbert H. Muller, "The City of Woe: Flannery O'Connor's Dantean Vision," *The Georgia Review* 23, no. 2 (1969): 206–13 (213).

21 Ludwin, "O'Connor's Inferno," 21.
22 Dante, *Divine Comedy of Dante Alighieri* (trans. Sinclair), 3:483.
23 See C. S. Lewis, *God in the Dock: Essays on Theology and Ethics*, ed. Walter Hooper (Grand Rapids: Eerdmans, 2014), 230–34.
24 Rahner, "Festival of the Future of the World," 180.
25 Rahner, *Spiritual Exercises*, 247.
26 Charles Williams, *The Figure of Beatrice: A Study in Dante* (Cambridge: D. S. Brewer, 1994), 231.
27 Dante, *Divine Comedy of Dante Alighieri* (trans. Sinclair), 3:485.
28 See Oliver Davies, "Dante's *Commedia* and the Body of Christ," in *Dante's "Commedia": Theology as Poetry*, ed. Vittorio Montemaggi and Matthew Treherne (Notre Dame, Ind.: University of Notre Dame Press, 2010), 161–79 (174).
29 Benjamin Myers, *Christ the Stranger: The Theology of Rowan Williams* (London: T&T Clark, 2012), 10.
30 Myers, *Christ the Stranger*, 11.
31 Karl Rahner, "The Task of the Writer in Relation to Christian Living," in *Theological Investigations*, vol. 8 (London: Darton, Longman, and Todd, 1971), 112–29 (119).

9 | Fire and Ashes

1   Gillian Rose, *Mourning Becomes the Law: Philosophy and Representation* (Cambridge: Cambridge University Press, 1996), 23.
2   Rose, *Mourning Becomes the Law*, 38.
3   Rose, *Mourning Becomes the Law*, 25.
4   Rose, *Mourning Becomes the Law*, 35–36.
5   Rose, *Mourning Becomes the Law*, 26.
6   Rose, *Mourning Becomes the Law*, 36.
7   Rose, *Mourning Becomes the Law*, 26.
8   Rose, *Mourning Becomes the Law*, 37.
9   See Kate Schick, *Gillian Rose: A Good Enough Justice* (Edinburgh: Edinburgh University Press, 2012).
10 Rose, *Mourning Becomes the Law*, 38.
11 For example, as David Nicholl learned during his time as rector at Tantur Ecumenical Institute in Jerusalem, it is usually if not always those who talk most about community-building who make life together most difficult. And it is very often "precisely the act by which it is hoped to create the perfect community" that generates distrust and devastating divisions. See David Nicholl, *The Testing of Hearts: A Pilgrim's Journey* (London: Darton, Longman & Todd, 1998), 34, 53.
12 This seems to shift, at least slightly, in *Love's Work* (New York: Vintage, 1997), which has as its epigraph St. Silouan's dark saying: "Keep your mind in hell, and despair not."

13 Carroll Stuhlmueller, *Rebuilding with Hope: A Commentary on the Books of Haggai and Zechariah* (Grand Rapids: Eerdmans, 1988), 53.

14 As Rose (*Mourning Becomes the Law*, 25) observes, "the bearing of the servant displays the political risk; her visible apprehension protects the complete vulnerability of her mourning mistress as she devotes her whole body to retrieving the ashes."

15 Jean-Louis Chrétien, *Hand to Hand: Listening to the Work of Art*, trans. Stephen E. Lewis (New York: Fordham University Press, 2003), 18–61. See also Susan Sontag, "The Aesthetics of Silence," in *Styles of Radical Will* (London: Penguin, 2009), 3–34.

16 Obery M. Hendricks Jr., *The Politics of Jesus: Rediscovering the True Revolutionary Nature of Jesus' Teachings and How They Have Been Corrupted* (New York: Doubleday, 2006), 113–21.

17 Willie James Jennings, *Acts* (Louisville, Ky.: Westminster John Knox, 2017), 34–35.

18 Daniela C. Augustine, *The Spirit and the Common Good: Shared Flourishing in the Image of God* (Grand Rapids: Eerdmans, 2019), 59, 65–66.

19 James Baldwin, *The Fire Next Time* (New York: Vintage, 1963), 39.

20 James Baldwin, *The Cross of Redemption: Uncollected Writings*, ed. Randall Kenan (New York: Pantheon, 2010), 201.

21 Charles Marsh, *Strange Glory: A Life of Dietrich Bonhoeffer* (New York: Knopf, 2014), 366.

22 Margaret Gaines, *Small Enough to Stop the Violence? Muslims, Christians, and Jews* (Cleveland, Tenn.: Cherohala Press, 2011).

23 Jane Liddell-King, "The Golden Calf," *European Judaism* 38, no. 2 (2005): 142–46 (146).

10 | More Than Many Sparrows

1 Amy Plantinga Pauw, *Church in Ordinary Time: A Wisdom Ecclesiology* (Grand Rapids: Eerdmans, 2017), 1.

2 Martin Buber, *The Letters of Martin Buber: A Life in Dialogue*, ed. Nahum N. Glatzer and Paul Mendes-Flohr, trans. Richard and Clara Winston and Harry Zohn (New York: Knopf Doubleday, 1991), 498.

3 Buber, *Letters of Martin Buber*, 223.

4 Buber, *Letters of Martin Buber*, 213–14.

5 Martin Buber, *The Prophetic Faith*, trans. Carlyle Witton-Davies (Princeton, N.J.: Princeton University Press, 2015), 235–44.

6 Susan Schreiner, "Calvin as an Interpreter of Job," in *Calvin and the Bible*, ed. Donald K. McKim (Cambridge: Cambridge University Press, 2006), 53–84 (58).

7 Schreiner, "Calvin as an Interpreter," 65.

8   Schreiner, "Calvin as an Interpreter," 69.

9   Schreiner, "Calvin as an Interpreter," 79.

10 Elie Wiesel, "In the Bible—Job Revisited," 92nd Street Y Elie Wiesel Archive, October 6, 1983, posted March 24, 2015, video, 1:18:01, https://www.youtube.com/watch?v=oimDq3yh0yw.

11 Quoted in Yuki Miyamoto, *Beyond the Mushroom Cloud: Commemoration, Religion, and Responsibility after Hiroshima* (New York: Fordham University Press, 2011), 131–32.

12 Rickie D. Moore, *The Spirit of the Old Testament* (Blandford Forum, Dorset, U.K.: Deo Publishing, 2011), 156.

13 Moore, *Spirit of the Old Testament*, 156.

14 Benjamin Pollock, *Franz Rosenzweig's Conversions: World Denial and World Redemption* (Bloomington: Indiana University Press, 2014).

15 Franz Rosenzweig, *The Star of Redemption* (Madison: University of Wisconsin Press, 2005), 437.

16 Frederick Christian Bauerschmidt, *The Love That Is God: An Invitation to Christian Faith* (Grand Rapids: Eerdmans, 2020), 34–36.

17 Johannes Baptist Metz, *Poverty of Spirit*, trans. John Drury (Mahwah, N.J.: Paulist Press, 1998), 21.

18 Dietrich Bonhoeffer, *Discipleship*, ed. Reinhard Krauss, trans. Barbara Green and Reinhard Krauss, *Dietrich Bonhoeffer Works* 4 (Minneapolis: Fortress, 2015), 173.

19 Buber, *Letters of Martin Buber*, 448.

20 Deborah Digges, "Vesper Sparrows," *Vesper Sparrows* (New York: Atheneum, 1986), 9–11.

Conclusion

1   Natalie Carnes, *Image and Presence: A Christological Reflection on Iconoclasm and Iconophilia* (Stanford, Calif.: Stanford University Press, 2018), 187.

2   Rowan Williams, "The Deflections of Desire: Negative Theology in Trinitarian Disclosure," in *Silence and the Word: Negative Theology and Incarnation*, ed. Oliver Davies and Denys Turner (Cambridge: Cambridge University Press, 2002), 115–35 (118).

3   Rowan Williams, *Christ the Heart of Creation* (London: Bloomsbury, 2018), 253.

4   Metz, *Poverty of Spirit*, 20.

5   Brennan O'Donnell, "A Conversation with Mary Karr," *Image* 56, https://imagejournal.org/article/conversation-mary-karr/.

6   Ian A. McFarland, *The Word Made Flesh: A Theology of the Incarnation* (Louisville, Ky.: Westminster John Knox, 2019), 8.

7   Metz, *Poverty of Spirit*, 26.

Bibliography

Alighieri, Dante. *The Divine Comedy of Dante Alighieri*. Vol. 3, *Paradiso*. Translated by John D. Sinclair. London: Bodley Head, 1946.

Allen, John L., Jr. "The Word from Rome." *National Catholic Register*, January 23, 2004. http://nationalcatholicreporter.org/word/word012304.htm.

Andrei Rublev (1966). Directed by Andrei Tarkovsky. Columbia Pictures.

Aquinas. *Summa Theologica*. https://www.newadvent.org/summa/.

Arbery, Will. *Heroes of the Fourth Turning*. New York: Samuel French, 2020.

Arendt, Hannah. *Love and Saint Augustine*. Edited by Joanna Vecchiarelli Scott and Judith Chelius Stark. Chicago: University of Chicago Press, 1996.

Auden, W. H. *For the Time Being: A Christmas Oratorio*. Edited by Alan Jacobs. Princeton, N.J.: Princeton University Press, 2013.

Auerbach, Erich. *Literary Language and Its Public in Late Latin Antiquity and in the Middle Ages*. Translated by Ralph Manheim. Princeton, N.J.: Princeton University Press, 1965.

———. *Mimesis: The Representation of Reality in Western Literature*. Translated by Willard R. Trask. Princeton, N.J.: Princeton University Press, 1953.

Augustine of Hippo. *City of God*. Translated by Henry Bettenson. London: Penguin, 1984.

———. *Letters*. Vol. 2. Translated by Wilfrid Parsons. Washington, D.C.: Catholic University of America Press, 1953.

Augustine, Daniela C. *The Spirit and the Common Good: Shared Flourishing in the Image of God*. Grand Rapids: Eerdmans, 2019.

Baldwin, James. *The Cross of Redemption: Uncollected Writings*. Edited by Randall Kenan. New York: Pantheon, 2010.

———. *The Fire Next Time*. New York: Vintage, 1963.

Barolini, Teodolinda. "Dante Alighieri." In *Women and Gender in Medieval Europe: An Encyclopedia*, edited by Margaret Schaus, 190–92. New York: Routledge, 2006.

Bauerschmidt, Frederick Christian. *The Love That Is God: An Invitation to Christian Faith*. Grand Rapids: Eerdmans, 2020.

Begbie, Jeremy S. "Beauty, Sentimentality and the Arts." In *The Beauty of God: Theology and the Arts*, edited by Daniel J. Treier, Mark Husbands, and Roger Lundin, 45–69. Downers Grove, Ill.: InterVarsity, 2007.

———. "The Sense of an Ending." The Veritas Forum, October 27, 2001. Video, 1:37:15. http://www.veritas.org/sense-ending/.

Berdyaev, Nicholas. *Dostoevsky*. Translated by Donald Attwater. New York: Meridian, 1957.

Billings, J. Todd. *The End of the Christian Life: How Embracing Our Mortality Frees Us to Truly Live*. Grand Rapids: Brazos, 2020.

Bonhoeffer, Dietrich. *Discipleship*. Edited by Reinhard Krauss. Translated by Barbara Green and Reinhard Krauss. *Dietrich Bonhoeffer Works* 4. Minneapolis: Fortress, 2015.

———. *Ethics*. Edited by Clifford J. Green. Translated by Reinhard Krauss, Douglas W. Stott, and Charles C. West. *Dietrich Bonhoeffer Works* 6. Minneapolis: Fortress, 2008.

The Book of Common Prayer. New York: Oxford University Press, 2005.

Booker, M. Keith. "The Dangers of Gullible Reading: Narrative as Seduction in García Márquez' *Love in the Time of Cholera*." *Studies in 20th & 21st Century Literature* 17, no. 2 (1993): 181–95.

Brenner, Wendy. "Strange Beads." *Oxford American* 81, Summer 2013. https://www.oxfordamerican.org/magazine/item/222-strange -beads.

Buber, Martin. *The Letters of Martin Buber: A Life in Dialogue*. Edited by Nahum N. Glatzer and Paul Mendes-Flohr. Translated by Richard and Clara Winston and Harry Zohn. New York: Knopf Doubleday, 1991.

———. *The Prophetic Faith*. Translated by Carlyle Witton-Davies. Princeton, N.J.: Princeton University Press, 2015.

Canonico, Domenic. "Good Friday: Creation Always Exists in Darkness." *Church Life Journal*, March 29, 2018. https://churchlifejournal.nd.edu/articles/good-friday-creation-always-exists-in-darkness/.

Carnes, Natalie. *Beauty: A Theological Engagement with Gregory of Nyssa*. Eugene, Ore.: Cascade, 2014.

———. *Image and Presence: A Christological Reflection on Iconoclasm and Iconophilia*. Stanford, Calif.: Stanford University Press, 2018.

———. *Motherhood: A Confession*. Stanford, Calif.: Stanford University Press, 2020.

Cep, Casey. "William Faulkner's Demons." *New Yorker*, November 23, 2020, https://www.newyorker.com/magazine/2020/11/30/william-faulkners-demons.

Chase, Steven. "Recollection." In *The New Westminster Dictionary of Christian Spirituality*, edited by Philip Sheldrake, 525–26. Louisville, Ky.: Westminster John Knox, 2005.

Chrétien, Jean-Louis. *The Ark of Speech*. Translated by Andrew Brown. London: Routledge, 2004.

———. *Hand to Hand: Listening to the Work of Art*. Translated by Stephen E. Lewis. New York: Fordham University Press, 2003.

Cooper, James Fenimore. *The Prairie*. London: Colburn and Bentley, 1832.

Davies, Oliver. "Dante's *Commedia* and the Body of Christ." In *Dante's "Commedia": Theology as Poetry*, edited by Vittorio Montemaggi and Matthew Treherne, 161–79. Notre Dame, Ind.: University of Notre Dame Press, 2010.

de Gruchy, John W. *Christianity, Art, and Transformation: Theological Aesthetics in the Struggle for Justice*. Cambridge: Cambridge University Press, 2001.

Denby, David. "Nailed." Review of *The Passion of the Christ*. *New Yorker*, February 22, 2004. https://www.newyorker.com/magazine/2004/03/01/nailed.

Dennis, David B. *Inhumanities: Nazi Interpretations of Western Culture*. Cambridge: Cambridge University Press, 2012.

Digges, Deborah. *Vesper Sparrows*. New York: Atheneum, 1986.

Donne, John. "Good Friday, 1613. Riding Westward." Poetry Foundation. https://www.poetryfoundation.org/poems/44103/good-friday-1613-riding-westward.

Dostoevsky, Fyodor. *The Idiot*. Translated by David McDuff. London: Penguin, 2004.

———. *The Notebooks for "The Idiot."* Edited by Edward Wasiolek. Translated by Katharine Strelsky. Mineola, N.Y.: Dover, 2017.

Du Mez, Kristin Kobes. *Jesus and John Wayne: How White Evangelicals Corrupted a Faith and Fractured a Nation.* New York: Liveright, 2020.

Ebert, Roger. "The Blink of a Life, Enclosed by Time and Space." Review of *The Tree of Life.* RogerEbert.com, June 1, 2011, https://www.rogerebert.com/reviews/the-tree-of-life-2011.

———. Review of *The Passion of the Christ.* RogerEbert.com, February 24, 2004. https://www.rogerebert.com/reviews/the-passion-of-the-christ-2004.

Elie, Paul. "Confronting Flannery O'Connor's Racism: A Response to Angela Alaimo O'Donnell." *Commonweal,* August 12, 2020, https://www.commonwealmagazine.org/confront-facts-oconnor.

———. "How Racist Was Flannery O'Connor?" *New Yorker,* June 15, 2020, https://www.newyorker.com/magazine/2020/06/22/how-racist-was-flannery-oconnor.

Eliot, T. S. "The Waste Land." In *The Waste Land and Other Poems,* edited by Christopher B. Ricks, 36. Orlando: Harcourt, Brace, 1997.

"Eulogy." *Better Things,* season 2 (October 19, 2017). Directed by Pamela Adlon. FX.

Evdokimov, Paul. *The Art of the Icon: A Theology of Beauty.* Translated by Fr. Steven Bigham. Redondo Beach, Calif.: Oakwood, 1990.

Fredriksen, Paula. "Augustine on God and Memory." In *Obliged by Memory: Literature, Religion, Ethics; A Collection of Essays Honoring Elie Wiesel's Seventieth Birthday,* edited by Steven T. Katz and Alan Rosen, 131–38. Syracuse, N.Y.: University of Syracuse Press, 2006.

Frei, Hans W. *The Identity of Jesus Christ: The Hermeneutical Bases of Dogmatic Theology.* Eugene, Ore.: Wipf & Stock, 1997.

Fujimura, Makoto. "Refractions 33: Georges Rouault—the First 21st Century Artist." October 17, 2009, https://www.makotofujimura.com/writings/refractions-georges-rouault/.

Gaines, Margaret. *Small Enough to Stop the Violence? Muslims, Christians, and Jews.* Cleveland, Tenn.: Cherohala Press, 2011.

Girard, René. "On Mel Gibson's *The Passion of the Christ.*" *Anthropoetics: The Journal of Generative Anthropology* 10, no. 1 (2004). http://anthropoetics.ucla.edu/ap1001/rggibson/.

Goodacre, Mark. "The Power of *The Passion*: Reacting and Overreacting to Gibson's Artistic Vision." In *Jesus and Mel Gibson's "The Passion of the Christ": The Film, the Gospels and the Claims of History*, edited by Kathleen E. Corley and Robert L. Webb, 28–44. London: Continuum, 2004.

Green, Chris E. W. *The End Is Music: A Companion to Robert W. Jenson's Theology*. Eugene, Ore.: Cascade, 2018.

———. "First and Last." *Fare Forward*, September 30, 2020. http://farefwd.com/index.php/2020/09/30/first-and-last/.

Greene, Graham. *The Power and the Glory*. New York: Penguin, 1991.

Greenwell, Garth. "Making Meaning: Against 'Relevance' in Art." *Harper's Magazine*, November 2020. https://harpers.org/archive/2020/11/making-meaning-garth-greenwell/.

Hansen, Ron. *Mariette in Ecstasy*. New York: HarperCollins, 1991.

Hart, David Bentley. *The Beauty of the Infinite: The Aesthetics of Christian Truth*. Grand Rapids: Eerdmans, 2004.

———. "The Gospel according to Melpomene: Reflections on Rowan Williams's *The Tragic Imagination*." *Modern Theology* 34, no. 2 (2018): 220–34.

Hauerwas, Stanley. "Character, Narrative, and Growth in the Christian Life." In *The Hauerwas Reader*, edited by John Berkman and Michael Cartwright, 221–54. Durham, N.C.: Duke University Press, 2001.

Hendricks, Obery M., Jr. *The Politics of Jesus: Rediscovering the True Revolutionary Nature of Jesus' Teachings and How They Have Been Corrupted*. New York: Doubleday, 2006.

Hesse, Hermann. *My Belief: Essays on Life and Art*. Edited by Theodore Ziolkowski. Translated by Denver Lindley. New York: Farrar, Straus and Giroux, 1974.

A Hidden Life (2019). Directed by Terrence Malick. Fox Searchlight Pictures.

Hill, Geoffrey. "Poetry as 'Menace' and 'Atonement.'" *University of Leeds Review* 21 (1978): 66–88.

Jennings, Willie James. *Acts*. Louisville, Ky.: Westminster John Knox, 2017.

———. "Overcoming Racial Faith." *Divinity* 14, no. 2 (2015): 5–9. https://divinity.duke.edu/sites/divinity.duke.edu/files/divinity-magazine/DukeDivinityMag_Spring15.WEB_.compressed.pdf.

Jenson, Robert W. "Christ as Culture 2: Christ as Art." *International Journal of Systematic Theology* 6, no. 1 (2004): 69–76.

———. "God, Space, and Architecture." *Response* 8 (1967): 157–62.

———. *On Thinking the Human: Resolutions of Difficult Notions*. Grand Rapids: Eerdmans, 2003.

———. *Systematic Theology*. Vol. 1, *The Triune God*. New York: Oxford University Press, 2001.

John of the Cross. *The Ascent of Mount Carmel*. In *The Collected Works of St. John of the Cross*, translated by Kieran Kavanaugh and Otilio Rodriguez. Washington, D.C.: Institute of Carmelite Studies, 2017.

John of Damascus. *Three Treatises on the Divine Images*. Translated by Andrew Louth. Crestwood, N.Y.: St. Vladimir's Seminary, 2003.

John Paul II. "Letter to Artists." April 4, 1999. http://www.vatican.va/content/john-paul-ii/en/letters/1999/documents/hf_jp-ii_let_23041999_artists.html.

Johnson, Luke Timothy. *The Acts of the Apostles*. Sacra Pagina 5. Collegeville, Minn.: Liturgical Press, 1992.

Jones, David. *The Anathemata*. London: Faber and Faber, 1952.

———. *Epoch and Artist*. London: Faber and Faber, 1959.

Jong, Jonathan. "Holbein's *Dead Christ*, Dostoevsky's *Idiot*, and Chalcedon's Jesus." St Mary Magdalen School of Theology, June 26, 2020. https://www.theschooloftheology.org/posts/essay/holbein-dostoevsky-christ.

Julian of Norwich. *Showings*. Translated by James Walsh. Mahwah, N.J.: Paulist Press, 1978.

Kermode, Frank. *The Sense of an Ending: Studies in the Theory of Fiction*. Oxford: Oxford University Press, 2000.

Kermode, Mark. "Drenched in the Blood of Christ." Review of *The Passion of the Christ*. *The Observer*, February 29, 2004. https://www.theguardian.com/theobserver/2004/feb/29/features.review7.

Kierkegaard, Søren. *Fear and Trembling/Repetition*. Edited and translated by Howard V. Hong and Edna H. Hong. Princeton, N.J.: Princeton University Press, 1983.

Laird, Martin. "Under Solomon's Tutelage: The Education of Desire in the *Homilies on the Song of Songs*." *Modern Theology* 18, no. 4 (2002): 507–25.

Lapin, Daniel. "Why Mel Owes One to The Jews." OrthodoxyToday.org, February 15, 2004. https://www.cbn.com/spirituallife/biblestudyandtheology/perspectives/passionmovie_rabbi.aspx.

Leithart, Peter J. *Shining Glory: Theological Reflections on Terrence Malick's "Tree of Life."* Eugene, Ore.: Cascade, 2013.

Lewis, C. S. *God in the Dock: Essays on Theology and Ethics*. Edited by Walter Hooper. Grand Rapids: Eerdmans, 2014.

Liddell-King, Jane. "The Golden Calf." *European Judaism* 38, no. 2 (2005): 142–46.

Louth, Andrew. *Introducing Eastern Orthodox Theology*. Downers Grove, Ill.: InterVarsity, 2013.

Ludwin, Deanna. "O'Connor's Inferno: Return to the Dark Wood." *The Flannery O'Connor Bulletin* 17 (1988): 11–39. http://www.jstor.org/stable/26669896.

MacKinnon, Donald. "Some Notes on the Irreversibility of Time." In *Explorations in Theology*, vol. 5, 90–98. Eugene, Ore.: Wipf and Stock, 2011.

Mamet, David. "They Think It's All Over: The Secret of a Great Ending—and the Movies That Are Lucky Enough to Have One." *The Guardian*, May 15, 2003. https://www.theguardian.com/film/2003/may/16/artsfeatures.davidmamet.

Maritain, Jacques. *Approaches to God*. Mahwah, N.J.: Paulist Press, 2015.

———. *Creative Intuition in Art and Poetry*. New York: Pantheon-Bollingen Foundation, 1953.

Marsh, Charles. *Strange Glory: A Life of Dietrich Bonhoeffer*. New York: Knopf, 2014.

Maximus Confessor. *Ambigua ad Thomam una cum Epistula secunda ad eundem*. Edited by Bart Janssens. Corpus Christianorum Series Graeca 48. Turnhout: Brepols, 2002.

———. *Opuscula theologica et polemica*. Edited by Jacques Paul Migne. Patrologia Graeca 91.85.d. 162 vols. Paris, 1857–1886.

McCarthy, Cormac. *The Road*. New York: Knopf, 2006.

McFarland, Ian A. *The Word Made Flesh: A Theology of the Incarnation*. Louisville, Ky.: Westminster John Knox, 2019.

Merton, Thomas. *No Man Is an Island*. New York: Harcourt & Brace, 1955.

Metz, Johannes Baptist. *Poverty of Spirit*. Translated by John Drury. Mahwah, N.J.: Paulist Press, 1998.

Metzger, Bruce M. *The Canon of the New Testament: Its Origin, Development, and Significance*. Oxford: Clarendon, 1987.

Milch, David. "Television's Great Writer, David Milch." MIT Communications Forum, 2006. Video, 1:23:30. February 17, 2016. https://techtv.mit.edu/videos/16086-television-s-great-writer-david-milch-mit-communications-forum.

Miyamoto, Yuki. *Beyond the Mushroom Cloud: Commemoration, Religion, and Responsibility after Hiroshima*. New York: Fordham University Press, 2011.

Moore, Rickie D. *The Spirit of the Old Testament*. Blandford Forum, Dorset, U.K.: Deo Publishing, 2011.

Morel, Lucas E. "Bound for Glory: The Gospel of Racial Reconciliation in Flannery O'Connor's 'The Artificial Nigger.'" *Perspectives on Political Science* 34, no. 4 (2005): 202–10.

Morrison, Toni. *Beloved*. New York: Random House, 2004.

Muller, Gilbert H. "The City of Woe: Flannery O'Connor's Dantean Vision." *The Georgia Review* 23, no. 2 (1969): 206–13.

Murphy, Debra Dean. "Alienated from Our Own Beauty." *Christian Century*, January 31, 2018. https://www.christiancentury.org/article/faith-matters/alienated-our-own-beauty.

Myers, Benjamin. *Christ the Stranger: The Theology of Rowan Williams*. London: T&T Clark, 2012.

Myers, Ched. "The Gospel of the Cross Confronts the Powers." In *Consuming Passion: Why the Killing of Jesus Really Matters*, edited by Simon Barrow and Jonathan Bartley, 61–73. London: Darton, Longman & Todd, 2005.

Neher, André. *The Exile of the Word: From the Silence in the Bible to the Silence of Auschwitz*. Translated by David Maisel. Philadelphia: Jewish Publication Society of America, 1981.

———. *They Made Their Souls Anew*. Translated by David Maisel. Albany: State University of New York Press, 1990.

Nicholl, Donald. *The Testing of Hearts: A Pilgrim's Journey*. London: Darton, Longman & Todd, 1998.

No Country for Old Men (2007). Directed by Joel and Ethan Coen. Miramax Films.

Noonan, Peggy. "It Is as It Was." *Wall Street Journal*, December 17, 2003, https://www.wsj.com/articles/SB122451994054350485.

O'Connor, Flannery. *The Complete Stories*. New York: Farrar, Straus and Giroux, 1971.

———. *The Habit of Being: Letters of Flannery O'Connor*. Edited by Sally Fitzgerald. New York: Farrar, Straus and Giroux, 1988.

O'Donnell, Brennan. "A Conversation with Mary Karr." *Image* 56. https://imagejournal.org/article/conversation-mary-karr/.

Pattison, George. "Idol or Icon? Some Principles of an Aesthetic Christology." *Literature and Theology* 3, no. 1 (1989): 1–15.

Pauw, Amy Plantinga. *Church in Ordinary Time: A Wisdom Ecclesiology*. Grand Rapids: Eerdmans, 2017.

Pfatteicher, Philip H. *Journey into the Heart of God: Living the Liturgical Year*. New York: Oxford University Press, 2013.

Pollock, Benjamin. *Franz Rosenzweig's Conversions: World Denial and World Redemption*. Bloomington: Indiana University Press, 2014.

Rahner, Karl. *Spiritual Exercises*. Translated by Kenneth Baker. New York: Herder and Herder, 1965.

———. *Theological Investigations*. Vol. 3, *The Theology of the Spiritual Life*. Translated by Boniface Kruger and Karl H. Kruger. London: Darton, Longman & Todd, 1967.

―――. *Theological Investigations*. Vol. 4, *More Recent Writings*. Translated by Kevin Smyth. London: Darton, Longman & Todd, 1966.

―――. *Theological Investigations*. Vol. 7, *Further Theology of the Spiritual Life I*. Translated by David Bourke. London: Darton, Longman & Todd, 1971.

―――. *Theological Investigations*. Vol. 8, *Further Theology of the Spiritual Life II*. Translated by David Bourke. London: Darton, Longman & Todd, 1971.

―――. *Theological Investigations*. Vol. 16, *Experience of the Spirit: Source of Theology*. Translated by David Moreland. London: Darton, Longman & Todd, 1979.

―――. *Theological Investigations*. Vol. 17, *Jesus, Man and the Church*. Translated by Margaret Kohl. London: Darton, Longman & Todd, 1981.

―――. *Theological Investigations*. Vol. 21, *Science and Christian Faith*. Translated by Hugh M. Riley. London: Darton, Longman & Todd, 1983.

Ricoeur, Paul. *Time and Narrative*. Vol. 1. Chicago: University of Chicago Press, 1984.

Ripatrazone, Nick. "*Mariette in Ecstasy*: Revisiting Ron Hansen's Outré, Erotic Catholic Novel, Twenty-Five Years Later." *The Paris Review*, November 22, 2016. https://www.theparisreview.org/blog/2016/11/22/mariette-in-ecstasy/.

Roark, David. "Terrence Malick and the Christian Story." RogerEbert.com, March 10, 2016. https://www.rogerebert.com/features/terrence-malick-and-the-christian-story.

Rose, Gillian. *Love's Work*. New York: Vintage, 1997.

―――. *Mourning Becomes the Law: Philosophy and Representation*. Cambridge: Cambridge University Press, 1996.

Rosenzweig, Franz. *The Star of Redemption*. Translated by Kathleen McLaughlin and David Pellauer. Madison: University of Wisconsin Press, 2005.

Ross, Maggie. "By Our Wounds We Are Healed." *Voice in the Wilderness* (blog), February 11, 2008. https://ravenwilderness.blogspot.com/2008/02.

Ruether, Rosemary Radford. "Sexism and Misogyny in the Christian Tradition: Liberating Alternatives." *Buddhist-Christian Studies* 34, no. 1 (2014): 83–94.

Salinger, J. D. *The Catcher in the Rye*. New York: Little, Brown, 1979.

Scarry, Elaine. *On Beauty and Being Just*. Princeton, N.J.: Princeton University Press, 2001.

Schick, Kate. *Gillian Rose: A Good Enough Justice*. Edinburgh: Edinburgh University Press, 2012.

Schreiner, Susan. "Calvin as an Interpreter of Job." In *Calvin and the Bible*, edited by Donald K. McKim, 53–84. Cambridge: Cambridge University Press, 2006.

Seitz, Matt Zoller. "'All Things Shining': The Films of Terrence Malick: *Badlands*." Originally published on Moving Image Source, a publication of Museum of the Moving Image. May 11, 2011. Video, 10:10. https://www.youtube.com/watch?v=NYfrI7EiXsU.

Shane (1953). Directed by George Stevens. Paramount Pictures.

Sharp, Ronald A. "George Steiner: The Art of Criticism, No. 2." *The Paris Review* 137 (1995). https://www.theparisreview.org/interviews/1506/the-art-of-criticism-no-2-george-steiner.

Slotkin, Richard. *Gunfighter Nation: The Myth of the Frontier in Twentieth-Century America*. New York: Macmillan, 1992.

———. *Regeneration through Violence: The Mythology of the American Frontier 1600–1860*. Norman: University of Oklahoma Press, 1973.

Smith, Barbara Herrnstein. *Poetic Closure: A Study of How Poems End*. Chicago: University of Chicago Press, 2007.

Smith, Maggie. *Good Bones*. North Adams, Mass.: Tupelo, 2017.

Solzhenitsyn, Alexandr [Aleksandr]. "Alexandr Solzhenitsyn—Nobel Lecture." NobelPrize.org, 1970. https://www.nobelprize.org/prizes/literature/1970/solzhenitsyn/lecture/.

Sontag, Susan. *Styles of Radical Will*. London: Penguin, 2009.

Steiner, George. *Real Presences*. New York: Open Road, 2013.

Stuhlmueller, Carroll. *Rebuilding with Hope: A Commentary on the Books of Haggai and Zechariah*. Grand Rapids: Eerdmans, 1988.

Swinton, John. *Dementia: Living in the Memories of God*. Grand Rapids: Eerdmans, 2012.

Tarkovsky, Andrey. *Sculpting in Time: Reflections on the Cinema*. Translated by Kitty Hunter-Blair. Austin: University of Texas Press, 1989.

Taylor, Mark C. "The Offense of Flesh." In *Mel Gibson's Bible: Religion, Popular Culture, and "The Passion of the Christ,"* edited by Timothy K. Beal and Tod Linafelt, 139–52. Chicago: University of Chicago Press, 2006.

———. "Time's Struggle with Space: Kierkegaard's Understanding of Temporality." *Harvard Theological Review* 66, no. 3 (1973): 311–29.

There Will Be Blood (2007). Directed by Paul Thomas Anderson. Paramount Vantage.

The Thin Red Line (1998). Directed by Terrence Malick. 20th Century Fox.

Thomas, R. S. *Collected Poems 1945–1990*. London: J. M. Dent, 1993.

———. *Laboratories of the Spirit*. London: Macmillan, 1975.

Thompson, Diane Oenning. "Problems of the Biblical Word in Dostoevsky's Poetics." In *Dostoevsky and the Christian Tradition*, edited by George Pattison and Diane Oenning Thompson, 69–99. Cambridge: Cambridge University Press, 2001.

To the Wonder (2012). Directed by Terrence Malick. Magnolia Pictures.

The Tree of Life (2011). Directed by Terrence Malick. Fox Searchlight Pictures.

Twain, Mark "Fenimore Cooper's Literary Offenses." Available online at http://xroads.virginia.edu/~Hyper/HNS/Indians/offense.html.

Updike, John. "Endpoint." *New Yorker*, March 9, 2009. https://www.newyorker.com/magazine/2009/03/16/endpoint.

———. *Telephone Poles and Other Poems*. London: Andre Deutsch, 1964.

Vodolazkin, Eugene. *Laurus*. Translated by Lisa C. Hayden. London: Oneworld, 2015.

Wall, Robert W., and Eugene E. Lemcio, eds. *The New Testament as Canon: A Reader in Canonical Criticism*. Sheffield, U.K.: JSOT Press, 1992.

Wells, Samuel. *Improvisation: The Drama of Christian Ethics*. Grand Rapids: Baker Academic, 2018.

Weil, Simone. "*The Iliad*, or the Poem of Force." *Chicago Review* 18, no. 2 (1965): 5–30.

Westen, John-Henry. "Gibson Film Realistic Portrayal of Christ." Review of *The Passion of the Christ. The Interim*, February 5, 2004. https://www.theinterim.com/issues/religion/gibson-film-realistic-portrayal-of-christ/.

Wetzel, James. "The Shrewdness of Abraham: Violence and Sexual Difference in a Paradigm of Monotheistic Faith." *Journal of Philosophy and Scripture* 3, no. 2 (2006): 25–30.

Wiesel, Elie. *Ani Maamin: A Song Lost and Found Again*. New York: Random House, 1974.

———. "In the Bible—Job Revisited." 92nd Street Y Elie Wiesel Archive. October 6, 1983. Posted March 24, 2015. Video, 1:18:01. https://www.youtube.com/watch?v=oimDq3yh0yw.

———. *Messengers of God: Biblical Portraits and Legends*. New York: Summit Books, 1976.

Williams, Charles. *The Figure of Beatrice: A Study in Dante*. Cambridge: D. S. Brewer, 1994.

Williams, Rowan. "The Bible Today: Reading and Hearing." Larkin-Stuart Lecture, Trinity and Wycliffe Colleges, Toronto, April 16, 2007.

———. *Christ the Heart of Creation*. London: Bloomsbury, 2018.

———. "A Conversation with Rowan Williams." Interview by John F. Deane. *Image* 80 (2014). https://imagejournal.org/article/conversation-rowan-williams/.

———. "A Curious Novel: Postmodernism and Holy Madness." TEDxOxBridge. July 5, 2016. Video, 14:44. https://www.youtube.com/watch?v=6MCB9JuLFzo.

———. "The Deflections of Desire: Negative Theology in Trinitarian Disclosure." In *Silence and the Word: Negative Theology and Incarnation*, edited by Oliver Davies and Denys Turner, 115–35. Cambridge: Cambridge University Press, 2002.

———. *Dostoevsky: Language, Faith, and Fiction*. Waco, Tex.: Baylor University Press, 2011.

———. "Grace, Necessity, and Imagination: Catholic Philosophy and the Twentieth Century Artist, Lecture 4: God and the Artist." Clark Lectures, Trinity College, Cambridge, March 3, 2005.

———. "Plague as Metaphor." In *Plagues*, edited by Jonathan L. Heeney and Sven Friedemann, 196–212. Cambridge: Cambridge University Press, 2017.

Wiman, Christian. *My Bright Abyss: Meditation of a Modern Believer*. New York: Farrar, Straus and Giroux, 2013.

Wright, Franz. *God's Silence*. New York: Knopf, 2008.

———. "The Raising of Lazarus." Poetry Foundation. https://www.poetryfoundation.org/poetrymagazine/poems/58345/the-raising-of-lazarus.

Wright, N. T. "Reading Paul, Thinking Scripture." In *Scripture's Doctrine and Theology's Bible: How the New Testament Shapes Christian Dogmatics*, edited by Markus Bockmuehl and Alan J. Torrance, 59–71. Grand Rapids: Baker Academic, 2005.

Index of Names

Index of Subjects

Index of Scripture